PRAYER

That Relieves

STRESS

And

WORRY

More praise for *Prayer That Relieves Stress and Worry*

"Helpful" hardly describes this book. "Life-saving" might be better. Simply sitting down and reading this book begins the process of relieving stress and worry. Deacon Eddie Ensley has written a soothing, centering book inviting the reader on a spiritual journey into a range of contemplative practices that can calm the inner and sometimes outer storms in our lives. He shows how each practice is appropriate to a particular kind of stress, briefly describes the biblical and historical tradition from which each practice comes, and provides simple, practical instruction for performing and growing in the practice ourselves."
—Dr. John McClure,
Vanderbilt University School of Religion

"The primary purpose (goal) of most books is simply to impart knowledge and this book *"Prayer That Relieves Stress and Worry,"* certainly does impart knowledge. However, Eddie Ensley's primary purpose is to impart deep, abiding, life changing faith and wisdom. And, he has gloriously achieved this goal. Every single verse, every single truth, and every single prayer, that is provided in this book will strengthen you and cause you to attain new depths in your relationship with the Lord."
—Richard G. Arno Ph.D.,
founder of National Christian Counselor's Association

"*Prayer That Relieves Stress and Worry* is an uncommon volume—practical and also profound. I was excited to read it, seeing at once how helpful it would be to me personally as well as professionally. It is a valuable contribution to anxiety management for Christian worriers. He has compiled a broad sample of scriptures, prayers, quotations and meditations that directly apply to familiar problems that cause excessive stress and worry.

With wise, compassionate understanding of how people struggle for deeper connection to God when they are anxious, and using language about praying that all Christians can relate to, Eddie Ensley shows how to create space and invite God to soothe worry and stress."
—Dr. Margaret Wehrenberg, licensed psychologist
Author of *The Anxious Brain and Stress Solutions:
10 Effective Strategies to Eliminate Your Stress*

"I have used the insights gained by reading Eddie Ensley's *Sounds of Wonder* for many years. His new book, *Prayer that Relieves Stress and Worry* will also be a wonderful blessing to those who read it. I found it most inspiring and helpful. I highly recommend it to everyone who is seeking peace from everyday stress and worry."
—Vinson Synan, professor of Divinity,
Dean emeritus Regent University School of Divinity

"*Prayer That Relieves Stress and Worry* is a beautiful book, a joy to read and ponder. I found my own stresses and worries melting away as I immersed myself in Eddie Ensley's touching stories and transforming prayers. It is the most meaningful book on prayer I have read in years. I will use the guided meditations in devotions before meetings and recommend the book for individuals and small groups in our church. It is filled with illustrations and stories that will enrich my preaching."

—John Sumwalt, United Methodist minister, author of *Shining Moments: Visions Of The Holy In Ordinary Lives*

"Soon into reading *Prayer That Relieves Stress and Worry*, I noticed my own stress from a hectic day begin to melt away. The Scripture verses and guided meditations at the end of each chapter are particularly comforting. In typical Ensley style, he makes it all real by telling wonderful stories to illustrate his message. I plan to use this book with our patients, who often find themselves overwhelmed with worry. This is a great resource to calm people down so healing can occur."

—Judy Esway, Chaplain Manager of Spiritual Care Mercy Gilbert Medical Center, author of *Letting Go*

"I cannot adequately express how much I appreciated your recent book, *Prayer That Relieves Stress and Worry*. You are one of those rare persons who have captured the way Jesus taught people... People crave intimacy with God. In your beautiful book you introduce hurting people to intimacy with Jesus as the way to inner healing, and the way of deepening our relationship with the divine. Congratulations on the beautiful work you have given to us all."
—Joseph F. Girzone, author of *The Joshua* novels

"A practical, compassionate guide to following the only prescription that truly relieves stress and worry—a closer relationship with Jesus, the Divine Healer and Great Physician."
—Louise Perrotta, author of *A Book of Grace-filled Days*

ALSO BY EDDIE ENSLEY

Visions, The Soul's Path to the Sacred

Prayer that Heals Our Emotions

Sounds of Wonder

BY EDDIE ENSLEY
AND ROBERT HERRMANN

Writing to be Whole: A Healing Journal

PRAYER
That Relieves
STRESS
And
WORRY

Eddie Ensley

CON✝EMPLATIVE
PRESS

Published in Fortson, GA by Contemplative Press.

This title may be purchased in bulk for educational, business, fundraising, or sales promotional use. For information, please email pmissions@charter.net

This book is not intended to offer professional advice or services to the individual reader. The suggestions in this book are not a substitute for visiting a physician, counselor or psychologist. All matters regarding health require medical supervision. Neither the author nor the publisher shall be liable for any loss or damages resulting from information or suggestions in this book.

The stories from this book that involve people other than the author make use of composites created by the author from his experience in ministry. Names and details of the stories have been changed, and any similarity between names and stories of individuals in this book to individuals known to readers is purely coincidental.

Scripture quotations unless otherwise indicated are from the New Revised Standard Version Bible ©1989 by the Division of Christian Education of the National Council of the Churches of Christ in the U.S.A., and are used by permission. All rights reserved.

ISBN# 978-0-9792775-4-2>

Printed in the United States of America

1 2 3 4 5 6 [   ] 08 07 06 05

Dedication

I dedicate this book to three people who have been such a great
support during the writing of this book: my cousins Betty Dollar and
Jane Galloway and my "cousin-in law" Morris Galloway.

In memory of my Aunt Genella Burke Crittenden,
who has been such an inspiration in my life.

TABLE OF CONTENTS

INTRODUCTION

Most everyone faces stress and worry. For some, it preoccupies their lives, leaving little room for enjoying this wonderful world God has given us. The present becomes difficult, the future worrisome, and the past is viewed through a darkened lens.

This book does not offer quick and easy psychological solutions or techniques to stress. None exist. Rather, the following chapters lead you to the one Source that can truly ease us, the magnificent and tender love of God.

The book guides you on a powerful journey of healing for yourself and those you care about. At the end of every chapter, specially selected Scriptures for prayerful reading will help drain you of stress and worry. The book includes stories drawn from people's lives to help nourish your mind and heart with the comforting realities of faith. Prayer journeys at the end of each chapter guide you into the refreshing depths of prayer

In this book you will encounter methods of prayer that calm you, so that your mind can stop racing and your head stop spinning. Practical, rock-solid advice, based in Scripture and Christian practice through the centuries, helps you cope with everyday pressures of life. Specific prayers at the end of each chapter bathe you in a warm caress. Learn ways of prayer that can be helpful in dissolving much of the irritability that often accompanies stress.

This book is written for all Christians—Catholic, Protestant, and Orthodox alike—and draws richly from all three traditions. Most chapters will end with Scripture for prayerful reading, starters for writing and as well as guided prayer journeys. All these pathways into God's rest are age-old spiritual disciplines. Upcoming chapters will give more detail on how to make these tried and proven ways of entering that rest, your own. Having said that, this book is not a substitute for professional help. If worry and stress severely affect you, it's important to seek out professional help.

Finally, I wish to thank the many people who helped with this book. Especially I want to thank my editor, Heidi Saxton, and the graphic design artist for the project, Jacinta Calcut. Thanks also to John Cobis who helped in the initial editorial phase—Deacon Robert Herrmann for his extensive editorial advice and organizational help. Thanks to Pat McArdle and my cousin Sue Towhey for feedback on the emerging manuscript. Thanks to Fr. Angelo Arrando for his encouragement, editorial help, and special input on the journaling sections. And last but not least, kudos to Joan Day for her excellent transcriptions and her prayerful support of the project.

When Jesus calls us to rest, he is calling us to more than a one-time act; he is calling us to a tender and continuous companionship. This closeness resembles the closeness between parents and child, between brothers and sisters, between the closest of friends. It reaches even beyond this human nearness, for according to St. Bernard, "he is more intimate to us then we are to ourselves."

ALEXANDER MACLAREN

1

Christ—The Friend Who Lifts Our Burdens

*"Accustom yourself to speak to God,
one-to-one, in a familiar manner
as to the dearest friend you have,
and who loves you best of all."*

ST. ALPHONSUS DE LIGUORI

WHEN I WAS LITTLE, MY AUNT GENELLA CRITTENDEN played an important role in shaping my spiritual life. She was a devout Baptist, raised in the parsonage of the Baptist Church in Odem, Georgia where her father was the minister. Her love of Christ and the Scriptures came from deep within her.

I have a vivid memory of the summer I was nine, spending two weeks with her and her husband, my Uncle Guthrie. When I came to them, I was as frightened and stressed-out as a nine-year-old boy could be. My mother was suffering from a severe stomach condition. Her weight had plummeted from her normal 130 pounds to a gaunt 96. I feared losing her.

There were other stressors as well. Earlier that year I had seen some awful cartoons that depicted God sending children to hell to be terrorized by demons. After that, I lived in constant fear that God would send me to hell also. A short time later, as Uncle Guthrie drove my Cousin Randy and me through Birmingham on the way to their home in Center Point, we witnessed a man crossing the street being hit by an oncoming car. I still remember the awful sight of the blood gushing from his head as he lay, dying, on the pavement.

All these disquieting events bore down heavily upon me. I was terrified of my mother dying. I shook inside with the prospect of being sent to hell. Scenes of the man bleeding on the pavement flashed before my eyes, followed by scenes of my dying in the same manner. Like most nine-year-olds, I kept most of this to myself.

Finally, one night as I lay in bed, tossing with worry, it became too much for me to handle alone. I had to tell. Hesitantly, I made my way to Aunt Genella's and Uncle Guthrie's bedroom and gently knocked on the door. A sleepy Aunt Genella opened the door, and the words poured out of me, "I'm sure I'm going to hell." I continued with an account of my other fears; my mother dying, and my fear of dying violently like the pedestrian I had seen.

Aunt Genella lovingly motioned for me to climb onto their bed where I sat nestled securely between them, my back propped up against the backboard with a pillow. More than fifty years have passed, so I've forgotten my aunt's and uncle's exact words, but their voices were full of warmth and comfort.

First of all, they assured me, God loved me and was not sending me to hell. Aunt Genella pulled out their large family Bible, then slowly and tenderly, pausing often, she read passages from Scripture that soothed and comforted. Fifty years later, I still recall those verses.

"Ask, and it will be given you. Search, and you will find. Knock, and the door will be opened for you.
For everyone who asks receives, and everyone who searches finds. For everyone who knocks, the door will be opened.

"Is there anyone among you who, if your child asks for bread, will give a stone? Or if the child asks for a fish, will give a snake? If you then, who are evil, know how to give good gifts to your children, how much more will your Father in heaven give good things to those who ask him!"

LUKE 7:7–11

After reading the passage, Aunt Genella said, "Eddie, by coming in here tonight, you are asking and seeking. Your heavenly Father won't respond by giving you a snake or a stone, or by sending you to hell. Tonight he offers you his comfort and peace." Then she opened her Bible again, and began calmly reading one Scripture after another.

Aunt Genella's slow reading of Scripture wove a web of safety around my soul.

Aunt Genella's slow reading of Scripture wove a web of safety around my soul. Through prayer, my stress and worry were greatly lessened. That calming time with Aunt Genella and the Scriptures was like the mountain of transfiguration for me. In the Holy light of the Scriptures, my fears diminished and I tasted something of the glory of God.

God can astound us with his power to relieve our stress and worry.

The world seemed different afterwards. Later in my life, I discovered that the slow, prayerful way Aunt Genella read Scripture was similar to a traditional way of praying Scripture called *lectio divina* or "Divine Reading," which opens our hearts to the embrace of God.

If you are reading this book, it is likely you are experiencing excessive stress, or because you carry worrisome burdens—you, or someone you care about. Perhaps you have turned to self-help books on stress or watched TV programs for advice on worry. Some of that information is helpful, but it can only go part of the distance in helping us with our heavy loads.

The overwhelming witness of Scripture, and two thousand continuous years of Christian tradition—Catholic, Protestant and Orthodox —tells us that in many unexpected ways, God can astound us with his power to relieve our stress and worry.

Christ promises us rest. In Matthew 11:28, he says "Come to me all you who are tired and heavy laden, and I will give you rest."

Closeness with God Lessens Stress

"As a mother delights in placing a child on her lap so as to feed and caress him, so our good God delights to treat [us] with the same tenderness, those who love without reserve and have placed all their hopes in God's goodness."

ALPHONSUS DE LIGOURI

Stress comes from many different sources: the pain of the past, the anxieties of the present, and the fears of the future. Also, the lack of a firm connection with God can stress us heavily. God built us body and soul for closeness to him; and we suffer both body and soul when that connection becomes impaired.

Some scientists say that we are hardwired to experience God; when we leave God out of our lives, that circuitry goes unnourished, causing stress. When we fail to give God time, or become too busy to speak and listen to him, we miss something vital to our well-being.

God's rest alone can calm the waters of our soul.

Mightier than secular relaxation techniques, God's rest alone can calm the waters of our souls.

St. Bernard teaches us that prayer helps break the circuit of feelings and thoughts that cause stress and worry. You no longer struggle inside, but experience the calm of God's love. His nearness lifts the weights of the problems on our shoulders.

St. Bernard of Clairvaux on the power of prayer:

"O good Jesus, from what great bitterness have you not freed me by your coming, time after time? When distress has made me weep, when untold sobs and groans have shaken me, have you not anointed (me)... with the ointment of your mercy and poured in the oil of gladness? How often has not prayer raised me from the brink of despair and made me feel happy in the hope of pardon? All who have had these experiences know well that the Lord Jesus is a physician indeed..."[1]

"Prayer refreshes ... the soul, as outer air refreshes the body. When we pray we feel stronger and fresher, as we feel physically and spiritually stronger and fresher when we walk in the fresh air."

JOHN OF KRONSTADT
RUSSIAN ORTHODOX PRIEST

Prayer Journeys

A Prayerful Reading

Read over the following Scripture passages slowly, with many pauses. Then read it again, two or three times. You will be surprised by how calming this can be. (For more information on this traditional form of praying the Scriptures, sometimes called *lectio divina*, go to page 27.)

When you pass through the waters, I will be with you
and through the rivers, they shall not overwhelm you;
when you walk through fire you shall not be burned,
and the flame shall not consume you.

(ISAIAH 43:2)

Can a woman forget her nursing child,
or show no compassion for the child of her womb?
Even these may forget, yet I will not forget you.
See, I have inscribed you on the palms of my hands.

(ISAIAH 49:16)

A Prayer of Childlike Intimacy

Dear Lord,

you know me far better than I know myself...

You understand me far better than I understand myself.

At times my life may be full of stress and worry.

When I pass through those stormy waters,

be with me and calm me,

and still the beating of my heart.

For in you, O Lord is deep rest,

perfect rest, all calm and all consolation.

I give you the worries of this day.

I give you the stresses of this day.

Keep me always near you,

for in your presence is calm.

In your presence is nurture and guidance.

And your strong arms, stretch out to hold me up

when I stumble.

Journal Time

Recording one's impressions and thoughts toward God is among the most time-honored of spiritual disciplines. Augustine in his "Confessions," Teresa of Avila's autobiography, Faustina's "Diary," and John Wesley's journal are all examples of this holy practice. Take a moment now to jot down—in whatever form suits you best—the thoughts that come as you enter in to this holy dialogue with God.

1. God consoles us in many varied ways. Can you think of at least one way in which God consoled you? Write about it.

2. Write a prayer of thanks to God for the times he has consoled you in the past.

All hail the power of Jesus' name!

Let angels prostrate fall;

bring forth the royal diadem,

and crown him Lord of all.

Bring forth the royal diadem,

and crown him Lord of all.

"All Hail the Power of Jesus Name"
EDWARD PERRONET, 1779

2

The "Jesus Prayer"—An Anchor
for a Restless Soul

Jesus told them,
"Pray then like this:
Our Father who art in heaven, hallowed be thy name. . ."
MATTHEW 6:9

IN THE SPRING OF 1996, the clamor of the phone shattered
my sleep. It was 6:00 A.M., and the panicky voice on the
other end of the line was my mother's. She told me that she
believed, but wasn't sure, that my father had just died. He
had been overcome with piercing chest pain and nausea, and
now appeared to have stopped breathing. Mother expected
the ambulance at any moment. She asked me to meet it
when it pulled in at the hospital emergency room. Mother
would remain at home.

As I drove toward the hospital, sickening dread filled me.
Daddy had been a calm and reassuring presence throughout
my life; I couldn't imagine my life without him. Sure, Daddy

had been seriously ill for years, yet he had lived to be eighty-five years old.

Still, that didn't take away the ache of losing him.

When I walked into the emergency room, I found that they had taken him to a backroom, where doctors were trying to revive him. I held little hope. As I waited, I feared my emotions would overpower me.

The name of Jesus is both sacred and powerful.

Later, when everything settled and I was back at home, I could surrender to my grief and break down, but not now. At the moment, if Daddy died, and it appeared likely he would, I had to hold it together. Too many important tasks lay ahead of me: calling the funeral home to arrange details, and informing relatives. Most of all, I needed to keep my composure to comfort Mother.

Still, desperately wanting to remain calm doesn't make it instantaneously happen. My thoughts turned in so many directions I couldn't even start a conversation with God.

All I could do was repeat, under my breath, a prayer I often pray, a shortened version of that ancient soothing prayer, the Jesus Prayer — "Jesus, Lord Jesus."

As I repeated the prayer over and over again, at first it sounded mechanical, just an act of my will. But soon the prayer began to replace my worried thoughts and pacify my troubled heart. God encircled me in his embrace. That peace didn't erase the wound of losing Daddy; I knew the grieving would still be difficult, but at least I wasn't alone now. A doctor emerged from the back and walked over to me and confirmed what I already knew. My father had died.

Whether it is a time of crisis or stress, or when you want to just tiptoe into God's presence; the Jesus Prayer can aid you. This biblically based early Christian prayer can warm your heart, and ease and relax your body.

Rooted in the Scriptures, the Jesus Prayer is primarily a prayer of the Spirit, because it addresses Jesus as Lord; as St. Paul tells us, "No one can say 'Jesus is Lord' except by the Holy Spirit" (1 Cor 12:3). Someone once asked me, "Isn't praying the Jesus Prayer one of those 'vain repetitions' Scripture warns against?" My answer was both quick and simple: "The name of Jesus is not vain."

> *"Write what you will, I shall not relish it unless it tells of Jesus…Jesus to me is honey in the mouth, music in the ear, a song in the heart.' Again, it is a remedy. Does one of us feel sad? Let the name of Jesus come into his heart and from there spring into his mouth, so that shining like the dawn it may dispel all darkness…*

> **Jesus is honey in the mouth, melody in the ear, a sense of joy in the heart.**
>
> BERNARD OF CLAIRVAUX

> *Does someone fall into sin? Does his despair even urge him to suicide? Let him but invoke this life-giving name and his will to live will at once be renewed.*

Bernard of Clairvaux
Fifteenth Sermon On the Song of Songs

Contemplating The Name of Jesus in Scripture

First, consider the beautiful simplicity of the prayer, and remember Jesus' command: In praying, we are *"not to heap up empty phrases as the heathen do' for they think that they will be heard for their many words. Do not be like them..."*
(MATT. 6:7–8).

The name of Jesus is both sacred and powerful. Devils are cast out in his name (Luke 10:17). *Prayers are answered* (John 14:13–14). Health may be restored (Acts 3:6–7). *Jesus, God enfleshed, is "the name which is above all other names," and so it is only fitting that "all beings should bend the knee at the name of Jesus"* (PHIL. 2:9–10).

The very words of the Jesus Prayer find their origin in Scripture. The blind man near Jericho cried, *"Jesus, Son of David, have mercy on me"* (Luke 18:38); and the publican cries for mercy pleading, *"Jesus, Son of David, have mercy on me"* (LUKE 18:38).

Are you experiencing a need for simple peace, for healing . . . the sense that your prayers are being heard? Are you in need of the merciful hand of God? Call out now upon his Son, the Word of God Incarnate. Say it now, and repeat it often . . . "Lord Jesus, have mercy on me."

"We must pray literally without ceasing - without ceasing; in every occurrence and employment of our lives. You know I mean that prayer of the heart which is independent of place or situation, or which is, rather, a habit of lifting up the heart to God, as in a constant communication with Him."

ELIZABETH ANN SETON

A Pilgrim's Heart is Strangely Warmed

The most famous book on the subject of the Jesus Prayer is *The Way of The Pilgrim* written by an anonymous, lame and destitute Russian peasant. Over the years this book became a spiritual classic that continues to sell well even today.[2]

The pilgrim yearned to find out what the Apostle Paul meant when he urged people to "pray without ceasing." A starets, or spiritual adviser and monastic elder, learned of the peasant's desire for understanding and taught him the Jesus Prayer, urging the peasant to pray this prayer frequently during the day. As the pilgrim prayed, a fiery flame of tender love burned in his heart. The prayer descended from his head to his heart, becoming "prayer of the heart." He also carried a Bible with him, and read a Gospel every day.

The prayer transfigured the created world around him.

> *The invocation of the Name of Jesus gladdened my way.*
>
> THE WAY OF A PILGRIM

He writes:

When I prayed in my heart, everything around me seemed delightful and marvelous. The trees, the grass, the birds, the air, the light seemed to be telling me that they existed for man's sake, that they witnessed to the love of God for man, that all things prayed to God and sang his praise.

In addition, the Jesus Prayer not only lifted the old pilgrim's burdens; it transformed his relations with his fellow human beings. He writes:

Again I started off on my wanderings. But now I did not walk along as before, filled with care. The invocation of the Name of Jesus gladdened my way. Everybody was kind to me. If anyone harms me I have only to think, "How sweet is the Prayer of Jesus!" and the injury and the anger alike pass away and I forget it all.

A Prayer of Comfort in Dark Times

Anna, an old friend, had just lost her social work job. Because of busyness, she forgot to file a required report, a grave error; and her agency terminated her. House and car payments needed to be made. Her daughter had just started college, and needed help with tuition. For three or four weeks after Anna lost her job, the stress weighed heavily. Her mind constantly turned over the possible dire outcomes.

Without an income, she could lose her house and car in two months.

She wanted to talk her worries over with God, but stress and worry clouded her mind and she couldn't get the conversation going. However, she had recently read about the Jesus Prayer, and decided now to try it out. She settled into her chair and then repeated a shortened version of the prayer "Jesus, Lord Jesus."

At first she was too conflicted even to cry. But after softly repeating the Jesus Prayer thirty minutes, the weight of her burden seemed to lessen. Serenity began to take over, and gentle tears of relief coursed down her face. As the Jesus Prayer warmed and calmed her heart, she began conversing with God again.

> *The Jesus Prayer warmed and comforted her heart.*

While prayer may not always solve every problem, prayer can calm the storms inside us so it becomes easier to make prudential decisions. Such was the case with Anna. She prayed the Jesus Prayer regularly, along with Scripture reading and conversational prayer, and these disciplines strengthened her resolve to tackle the issues she faced. She talked with local contacts about other job possibilities. She called different agencies and local colleges. Finally, she landed a job as an instructor teaching social work at a nearby college and added to that part-time work at a private agency. She made enough to make the house and car payments, plus help with her daughter's college tuition.

Through the centuries, Christians in the midst of stress have turned to prayers such as the Jesus Prayer to ease them into stillness. The exact wording of the prayer is not as important as the intention behind it. Orthodox Christians, who have a long history of praying the Jesus Prayer, use a variety of forms. Eastern Christians view any invocation of the Holy Name of Jesus as an authentic Jesus Prayer.

> *God loves every one of us as if we were the only ones he had to love.*
>
> AUGUSTINE

Over the years the prayer crystallized into the phrase, "Lord Jesus Christ, Son of God, have mercy on me a sinner." However, the Jesus Prayer and similar prayers, in themselves, are not recited simply as a means to attain stress relief. Rather, the prayer invites God into the far reaches of the soul. What calms us, stills us, and gives us rest is his presence within.

How to Pray the Jesus Prayer

The simplest forms of praying the prayer usually work best. The earliest form of the prayer was simply to repeat lovingly the word "Jesus" over and over again.

Many people simply pray, "Jesus, Lord Jesus." Others quote Scripture, such as Philippians 2:11: "Jesus is Lord, to the glory of God the Father" (Phil 2:11).

You can pray the prayer anytime and in any circumstance: while falling asleep, waiting in the grocery line, taking a walk, or riding in a car. Even though you can pray anywhere and anytime, be sure to take fifteen to twenty minutes of quiet time to pray the Jesus Prayer so the prayer can tenderly warm the interior parts of your heart.

Most people offer the Prayer while seated. Find a chair that is not too hard: otherwise you will fidget with discomfort. Use a chair that is soft, but at the same time supports your back in an upright position.

Start by surrendering to God. Begin your time of prayer by first abandoning yourself and your prayer time into God's care. Ask him to take charge. Perhaps say a prayer like this: "Lord, I turn this prayer time over to you. Do with me what you will." Others prefer the Scriptural prayer: "Father, into your hands I commend my spirit" (Lk 23:46).

After you have surrendered your prayer time into God's hands, begin softly saying your Jesus Prayer. Say it out loud, if possible; or if not, at least under your breath.

When your thoughts wander ... We all have busy attics. Wandering thoughts are part of being human. I'm sure Jesus had wandering thoughts when he prayed; he was human, after all.

Wandering thoughts in prayer are not sinful; they are natural. You didn't will to have these thoughts; they came unbidden.

Wandering thoughts in prayer can be a symptom of pent-up stress; the thoughts were with us all along, suppressed, pushed down and locked inside. Think of what happens when a capped bottle of cola is shaken. The bottled-up fizz creates great pressure inside the bottle. Finally, when the cap is taken off, the fizz spews out the top, relieving the pressure. Our busyness and preoccupations cap the thoughts within us. When we take time of the Jesus Prayer, we take the cap off and the thoughts, which were with us all along, but hidden emerge into our consciousness.

Gently turn your thoughts back to prayer. Don't add to your stress by becoming angry with yourself. After all, the last act of your will before a random thought emerged was an act of loving God, saying the Jesus Prayer. You didn't suddenly say, "I'll interrupt my prayer and choose to have a wandering thought instead." Remember, you surrendered yourself to God for the length of your prayer time. What happens in that prayer time is God's business.

When a wandering thought interrupts your Jesus Prayer, the best way to handle it is simply to notice it, then let it pass by. Next, return to saying your Jesus Prayer. Don't focus on the thought. Think of a wandering thought as a bird that flies by in the air; you notice it and let it fly away, but you don't make a nest for it.

If in the course of a thirty-minute prayer time, wandering thoughts interrupt your prayer a hundred times and you return to saying your prayer each time, you have made a hundred separate acts of loving God.

FR. WILLIAM MENNINGER

Lovingly rest in God. After you finish saying your Jesus Prayer, rest in the love of God. More than anything else God simply wants to love us. And as Augustine said, "He loves every one of us as if we were the only ones he had to love." Let your heart sink into the ease of silent adoration.

PRAYER JOURNEYS

A Prayerful Reading
Read over the following Scriptures, slowly and prayerfully, with long pauses. Read them out loud if possible.

Blessed be the God and Father of our Lord Jesus Christ,
the Father of mercies and God of all comfort,
who comforts us in all our affliction,
so that we may be able to comfort those
who are in any affliction,
with the comfort with which we ourselves
are comforted by God.
For as we share abundantly in Christ's sufferings,
so through Christ we share abundantly in comfort too
(2 CORINTHIANS 1:3–5, RSV.)

Let the same mind be in you that was in Christ Jesus,
who, though he was in the form of God,
did not regard equality with God
as something to be exploited,
but emptied himself,
taking the form of a slave,
being born in human likeness.
And being found in human form,
he humbled himself
and became obedient to the point of death—
even death on a cross.

Therefore God also highly exalted him
and gave him the name
that is above every name,
so that at the name of Jesus
every knee should bend,
in heaven and on earth and under the earth,
and every tongue should confess
that Jesus Christ is Lord,
to the glory of God the Father

(PHIL. 2:5–11).

A Prayer to the Holy Name

Dear Lord,
may your holy name ever be on our tongues,
warm our hearts and quiet our minds.
For the name Jesus holds more power
than the entire universe.
In your name is comfort,
consolation, peace and stillness.
The name of Jesus calms our storms,
smooths our pathways,
brightens our lives,
stills our hearts.

Journal Time

1. Describe some of the stresses and worries you have felt over the last week or so. Just naming them on paper lessens their power.

2. Write a prayer surrendering your worries and stresses to Christ.

[1] St. Bernard, Song of Songs II page136.

[2] You may find excerpts of the book online at
http://landru.i-link-2.net/shnyves/Prayer_without_Ceasing.html

"If the practice of lectio divina is promoted with efficacy, I am convinced that it will produce a new spiritual springtime in the Church."

POPE BENEDICT XVI
NOVEMBER 16, 2005

"Meditation is a settled exercise of the mind for a further inquiry of the truth... Meditation pulls the latch of the truth, and looks into every closet, and every cupboard, and every angle of it. It labors to affect the heart."

BIBLICAL ILLUSTRATOR

3

How Scripture Can Ease Conflict

How sweet are your words to my taste,
sweeter than honey to my mouth!
Your word is a lamp to my feet
and a light to my path.
PSALM 119:103–105

When we open God's book, and meditate upon its contents,
and endeavor to profit in the study of it,
His presence breathes in every page, and speaks words of mercy,
warning, and encouragement to our souls.
ALEXANDER MACLAREN

FOR A FULL WEEK I HAD DREADED GIVING A RETREAT to the faculty of a Midwestern Catholic girl's school. I kept hoping they would cancel, but they didn't.

Five minutes into my first talk of the morning, I knew my fears were justified and the retreat was in trouble. Grim, stony faces, glared at me. The audience reminded me of a pot of water on the edge of boiling over. I already knew the reason for the discontent. A week earlier the pastor had called to tell me that the faculty was in meltdown.

The new principal had been pushing hard for the teachers to improve their teaching skills and lesson plans. A number of the faculty reacted with resentment. At one faculty meeting, the tension erupted in a shouting match between faculty loyal to the new principal and those resenting her.

> *Benedict called lectio divina listening "with the ear of our hearts."*

Several teachers even became insubordinate to the new principal. Afterward, unfounded rumors flew that the board would fire several of the teachers or replace the principal.

During lunch break a handful of teachers on both sides of the dispute unburdened themselves to me. I had planned to give a talk on prayer for the first afternoon conference. But given the current state of the faculty, I doubted that the talk would be well received. As I mulled over what to present in that afternoon conference, I remembered how my Aunt Genella's prayerful reading of Scripture had encircled me in calm and safety when I was nine.

Suddenly, it came to me: Instead of *talking* about prayer, we needed to *pray*. Most of all, we needed to pray Scripture. That afternoon we needed words and thoughts from beyond ourselves to penetrate our hearts.

That afternoon, I first gave a brief introduction to an age-old way of prayerfully reading the Scriptures. While *lectio divina* is primarily for individual prayer, it can also be adapted for use by groups.

Next, I asked everyone to close their eyes. I began playing a slow, prayerful CD of Pacabel's "Canon in D" in the background. After the music had played a minute or two, we took about ten minutes to say the Jesus Prayer.

In the calm and quiet I slowly started reading from 1 Corinthians 13, pausing in the stillness when I felt the gentle touch of the Spirit move over the group. It was clear from their faces that the group was settling into a deep state of prayer.

Then I read the chapter once more, slowly and with pauses, giving time for the words to sink in. This time I repeated words and phrases that seemed "anointed" by a special touch of the Spirit.

"Love is patient," I repeated slowly, then paused in a long silence.

"Love is kind. It is not irritable or resentful." I paused again.

Next I read from the thirteenth chapter of the Gospel of John, the passage that describes Jesus washing the feet of the disciples. In the second reading of the passage, I slowly repeated the phrase "wash one another's feet."

When I had finished the reading, we took ten minutes of silent prayer.

After a few moments, one of the middle-aged teachers spontaneously broke the quiet. Tears coursing down her face, her voice choked as she addressed the group. "I regret so much my outburst at the last faculty meeting." She turned to the principal. "You didn't deserve the cruel words I aimed at you. You are a decent human being who loves the students as much as I do."

The principal walked over and embraced the teacher, tears streaming from her eyes, too. The principal addressed the group as well. "Please forgive me, I could certainly be far more sensitive to your feelings and opinions as I implement these new policies."

Then one teacher after the other expressed regret and the strong wish for the faculty to be reconciled. The presence of God was so thick, there was hardly a dry eye in the room.

"The commonplaces of religion are the most important. Everybody needs air, light, bread, and water. Meditate, then, upon the things most surely believed, and ever meditate until the dry stick of the commonplace truth puts forth buds and blossoms like Aaron's rod… This great truth will shine into our gloom like a star into a dungeon."

ALEXANDER MACLAREN

Getting to the Heart of Scripture

If we are to draw close to the heart of God, we must be willing to listen for his still, small voice (1 Kings 19:9–18). "They are the faint, murmuring sounds . . . [of] God's word for us, God's voice touching our hearts," observes Luke Dysinger, O.S.B., who describes *lectio divina* as "accepting the embrace of God."

Often we want to read the Scriptures to obtain knowledge and meaning. We can never do without Bible study; the Bible is divine revelation, after all. For Bible study we need to read Scripture in context and often consult good commentaries. *Lectio divina* is a different way of reading; a more intimate reading of Scripture, a reading with the heart. *Lectio divina* is also a way of prayerful listening, for the soft, quiet voice of God. Benedict called *lectio divina* listening "with the ear of our hearts."

Your heart will instinctively apply the word or phrase to your life.

So, how does one begin? There are four simple steps.

1. Begin with prayer. Before you actually begin, take time to grow quiet in prayer, perhaps using the Jesus Prayer. Take deep breaths and allow your heart to settle into a deep calm.

2. "Tolle, lege": Take up and read. Next is the *lectio* or reading. Pick a passage of Scripture to read slowly. You may want to read it several times, each time a little more slowly and with longer pauses between lines and phrases, enabling the meaning to sink deep into the soul. Usually most people read each passage at least two times.

Consciously slow your reading. The speed with which we read newspapers or articles on the Web is not appropriate for *lectio divina.* One of the best ways to slow yourself down is to quietly read the passage aloud. Some people feel uncomfortable reading aloud, but give it a try. If you still feel uncomfortable reading aloud, just repeat the words slightly under your breath, move your tongue but enunciate the words just under your breath. Read it slowly. Savor it. Let the feelings of the scripture get inside you.

3. *Ponder, ruminate, and meditate.* Finally, we move to *meditatio* or meditation. When a phrase resonates within us as we are reading, we "ruminate" on it, just like an animal chews its cud. We ponder it with the heart. When you come to such a word or phrase, repeat several times slowly After you have savored and repeated the word or phrase, rest in stillness a moment as long as it seems right to you.

> *It is in the silence that we allow God to do what he wants to do most of all, simply love us.*

This rest is a wordless basking in the presence of the one who loves us without measure. Your heart will instinctively apply the word or phrase to your life. When you come to a phrase or word that touches you, repeat it over and over again very slowly, it will take on a kind of anointing.

For instance, if you are reading Psalm 23, "The Lord is My Shepherd, I shall not want, he makes me to lie down in green pastures … he restores my soul," the phrase "restores my soul" may seem particularly significant, something to savor. Just repeat that over and over, as long as the grace of the moment lasts.

4. *Deepen your contemplation.* When you are ready, close your Bible and close your eyes. It is the time for intimate conversation with God, verbal prayer. A phrase or a word

may so inspire you that you offer a prayer to God, and then perhaps hear his wordless, "still small voice."

Don't worry about having the "right" words to offer God. It is in the silence that we allow God to do what he wants to do most of all, simply love us. This is a wordless prayer, a resting, a stillness. Such prayer is a gift of God, an invitation to intimate union. Anyone who has been in love knows that there are moments of wordless communion when hearts seem as one.

This may seem complicated, but it really isn't. The parts of *lectio divina* don't necessarily come in exact set stages. For instance, you might feel an inspiration to offer a prayer early in the reading; if you do, stop and pray.

You may feel yourself drawn to repeat a word or phrase and ruminate over it. Do so at anytime.

You may be drawn in to the loving stillness of contemplation at any moment. If you do, stop and rest silently in God's presence. You will know when it is time to begin reading passage again.

Finding Healing in the Stillness

A year after the death of her husband, Lucille was still in the grips of crisis. She and her husband had both been in their sixties when he died. For two decades they had taught the techniques of good communication within marriage to hundreds of people on retreat weekends, called Marriage Encounter.

Always genuinely in love with each other; their work with

Marriage Encounter simply deepened their bonds and their love for one another. Countless times they gave talks about how good communication and spirituality helped keep marriages close.

> *Anyone who has been in love knows that there are moments of wordless communion when hearts seem as one.*

That made her husband's death particularly tragic for Lucille. She had never thought or planned to live alone. Prayer was especially difficult; they had always taken their quiet times together, and she was not use to praying alone. She carried a weight of grief and stress.

Lucille had read about *lectio divina* (prayerful reading) in a magazine, and she decided to try it. She picked a passage from Isaiah 40, and slowly began reading to herself, savoring each word.

> *"Comfort, my people, says your God.*
> *Speak tenderly to Jerusalem and cry to her*
> *that her warfare is ended."*

Lucille read over the passage two or three times slowly before something truly touched her: "Speak tenderly to Jerusalem …"

Delicately she began repeating the phrase. "Speak tenderly to Jerusalem …" Gradually she felt led to shorten the phrase, praying, "Speak tenderly … speak tenderly … speak tenderly."

A gentle love quietly welled up within her. She rested for

a moment in the silence of that love. "Speak tenderly to me, Oh Lord. Speak tenderly to me." She slowly repeated that prayer until her heart quieted. She then rested in the silence for five or ten minutes.

Later, she said to me, "praying that Scripture helped me to feel, for the first time since my husband died, that God loved me tenderly." As she daily prayed this way, an abiding sense of God's presence filled her heart. Of course *lectio divina* did not take away the pain from the loss of her husband, but it did give her a sense that when she prayed, she was not alone. "I know I will always grieve for him until my own death," she said to me. "But I know for sure now that there is indeed someone who holds me close beside my husband, God. And I can converse with him at any moment and I can hear God converse with me, through Scripture."

Dear Lord, at times my heart is troubled and afraid.
There are times I stumble and can't find my way.
Take my hand, then, and calmly lead me.
May your words still me.
May your Scriptures embrace me, reassure me,
bring me calm.
For your word is a lamp to my feet,
a tender embrace of my heart,
a pathway for body and soul. Amen.

Prayer Journeys

A Prayerful Reading (*lectio divina*)

Read these passages slowly,
frequently pausing to listen for the still, small voice of God.

Do not let your hearts be troubled.
Believe in God, believe also in me.
In my Father's house there are many dwelling places.
If it were not so, would I have told you that I go to prepare a
place for you?
And if I go and prepare a place for you,
I will come again and will take you to myself,
so that where I am, there you may be also...
Peace I leave with you; my peace I give to you.
I do not give to you as the world gives.
Do not let your hearts be troubled,
and do not let them be afraid

(JOHN 14:1–3, 27).

God is our refuge and strength,
a very present help in trouble.
Therefore we will not fear, though the earth should change,
though the mountains shake in the heart of the sea;
though its waters roar and foam,
though the mountains tremble with its tumult

(PSALM 46:1–3).

Journal Time

1. When you hear the words, "God is a refuge and strength . . ." do these words remind you of any personal experiences? Write about them.

2. If God wrote a letter to you about your worries and stresses, what do you think he would say?

"Even now, I beseech you, lift up the eye of the mind, even now imagine the choirs of Angels, and God the Lord of all there sitting, and His Only-begotten Son sitting with Him on His right hand, and the Spirit present with them, and Thrones and Dominions doing service, and everyman of you and every woman receiving salvation. Even now your ears ring, as it were, with that glorious sound, when over your salvation the angels shall chant. Blessed are they whose iniquities are forgiven, and whose sins are covered: when like stars of the Church you shall enter in, bright in the body and radiant in the soul."

CYRIL OF JERUSALEM (FOURTH CENTURY)

4

The Solace of Sacred Imagination

He said to them,
"Why are you afraid? Have you no faith?"
MARK 5:40

THE SUN SHOWN BRIGHTLY IN MEMPHIS the day we started the last parish mission in the spring of 2005. Afterward, I would return home and relax for several months until mission season began again in the fall.

As I napped the first afternoon there, the cell phone rang. My Cousin Edward, his voice grimly resigned, told me that Aunt Genella's health had suddenly deteriorated. Her doctor gave her two days, at the most, to live. A blood clot had blocked off circulation in her leg. The only option the doctor offered was amputation; however, considering her overall medical condition, he was afraid the operation would likely kill her.

Aunt Genella quickly settled the matter. "I don't want to be cut on again," she told the doctor. She was fully alert; she knew she was dying, and was completely prepared for what was ahead.

Denial and aching loss flooded my soul. Before the awful news, it hadn't occurred to me that the time might come when Aunt Genella would no longer be there. Sure, she was eighty-seven, and a stroke had paralyzed her two years before. But her mind remained quick, and her love of God still brightened her personality. She read several novels a week, and Edward and his wife Doris took her out to lunch often. Over that last year she called me at least two or three times a month, wanting to know everything about my missions and my writing. She encouraged and comforted me when I needed it. I had visited her just a few weeks before the Memphis mission. Vivacious, full of humor, she made me laugh as she regaled me with stories from long ago.

Early the next day Edward called again. Aunt Genella had died. She hadn't lived the full two days, after all. Inside, I was shattered. How could I finish the mission when I felt such intense grief? How could I preach about inner peace when I had so much tumult within?

I knew what Aunt Genella would do; she would open her Bible. So I pulled mine out. I turned to Mark 4:35–41, the passage that describes Jesus calming the sea. I read each word slowly, just as Aunt Genella had read to me when I was nine. I read Jesus' words when he calmed the water.

"Peace, be still."

Leisurely I repeated them over and over again with long pauses, to let the words descend into my heart. I repeated the same process with the next phrase:

"Why are you so afraid?"

Stillness enveloped me. Soon I settled down enough for brief conversational prayer. "Dear Lord, please help me, please keep my heart quiet."

Next, I sat in the chair and I imagined Jesus sitting next to me. My imagination was fuzzy just then, but just having a sense of the scene was enough. Jesus wore a long flowing robe, and light emanated from him. He took my hand in his. My fingers traced the wound where the nail had been.

> *In Christian meditation we don't blank our minds or try by our own wills to achieve some exalted state. Instead, we center our hearts on God.*

I felt the warmth of his healing flow from his hand into mine. The warmth passed through my hand into my arm. Then spread to my shoulders, into my chest, surrounding my heart, restoring peace. In my imagination, Jesus began slowly repeating the words to me, "Peace, be still."

For a moment, I tasted that "peace that passes understanding" she talked about. Scenes of fun times with her paraded through my mind. I still feel Aunt Genella's loss, and I know I always will, but I do have the blessed memories of her and God's peace to help me in my grieving.

Imagine Jesus Quieting the Storm

Several months later, just after I finished a talk on God's peace at a Midwest mission, a middle age woman, Jane, approached me. "I worry so much," she said. Immediately, her worries poured out of her mouth in a torrent. Obviously she needed more than the two or three minutes I had available to talk with her. I suggested that we meet in a church office the next day.

You can find imagination prayer in the Bible and throughout all the Christian centuries.

When we met, I soon found that Jane worked full-time at nights, while attending school to earn her nursing degree. She made a C on a mid-term and feared failing. Her worries so distracted her, she feared losing her job. She spoke of even more imaginary "scenarios of doom."

As I listened to her, I thought imagination prayer could help her. I wanted her to turn her active imagination from harmful scenes to positive ones. I pulled out the Bible and prayerfully read the 23rd Psalm to her to help her calm down. Then I read the story of Jesus calming the storm that had so helped me after Aunt Genella's death.

I said to Jane, "Imagine the scene of Jesus quieting the storm. Imagine yourself in the boat with Jesus and the disciples. Huge waves toss the boat around. Rain pounds down on you. The wind howls. Then the disciples wake Jesus and he says 'Peace, be still.' Then the storm ceases, replaced by calm. Picture Jesus coming to you in the boat, taking your hand. His love and peace fill you, and your stress begins to leave you.

"Now Jesus whispers, 'Peace. Be still,' just to you." I asked her to rest a while in the stillness. After we closed, her face looked serene and drained of stress. She looked at me, and then said, "When Jesus said, 'Peace, be still,' my worries greatly lessened."

I reminded her that imaginative prayer doesn't eliminate the reality of life's stresses, but it can give us the greater ability to mange those stresses. We can use the imagination to conjure up distressful scenes. Or we can use our imaginations to center on God and God's peace. Jane still needed to face her problems. Now, however, she possessed another prayer tool to carry her into the loving welcome of God's arms.

Is Imaginative Prayer Scriptural?

The word *meditate* frightens some Christians. They think of fake gurus in robes coming from the east beating drums and selling meditation for a price. Let's not let this popular but mistaken idea stop us from meditating. Meditation is an ancient Christian practice found and written about in both the Protestant and Catholic traditions alike. In Christian meditation we don't blank our minds or try by our own wills to achieve some exalted state. Instead, we center our hearts on God.

Guided meditation is really a form of prayer leading to contemplative stillness; it is not some import into Christianity. You can find imagination prayer in the Bible and throughout all the Christian centuries.

Some of the psalms are imaginative meditations, especially Psalm 23. The words carry anyone who prays this psalm into green pastures, still waters, leads through the valley of the shadow of death, where "Thou art with me."

Early Christians used imaginative meditation. In the fourth century, Cyril of Jerusalem used guided imagery in the lectures he used to prepare people to enter the Church. Scribes recorded the lectures and scholars preserved them to this day.

In the Protestant and Orthodox traditions, guided meditations are found primarily in hymns such as the beloved Gospel hymn, "In the Garden." Through these meditations, we discipline the imagination, causing it to dwell on eternal themes rather than present circumstances, real or illusory. In this way, God is able to break in and offer comfort and consolation at our weakest and most fearful moments.

I come to the Garden alone, while the dew is still on the roses,
And the voice I hear falling on my ear, the Son of God discloses.
And he walks with me and he talks with me,
And he tells me I am his own.
And the joys we share as we tarry there,
None other has ever known.

"IN THE GARDEN" (1912) BY C. AUSTIN MILES

Why a Picture Is Worth a Thousand Words

Imagination is the language of the unconscious. Before we could think and speak, we thought in images. At nighttime we dream in images. Often athletes use visualization, picture themselves performing well and find that their imagination enhances their performance.

For the most part, our imagination is undisciplined. We fall prey to images we receive from our culture and especially through the media. Edward Halowell, a Christian psychiatrist that teaches at Harvard Medical School, calls constant worry "a disease of the imagination." He continues, "The imagination is a two-edged sword ... you can use it to dream of good stuff, or you can use it to dream up bad stuff."

In Christian meditation, we discipline the imagination and use it to open ourselves to the God of Scripture.

> *Pictures go straight to the heart in a way words never can. That is why Jesus told stories. He gave people verbal pictures to reach the inmost places of their souls.*

Pictures go straight to the heart in a way words never can. That is why Jesus told stories. He gave people verbal pictures to reach the inmost places of their souls. In the Sermon on the Mount, Jesus said, "Look at the birds of the air; they neither sow nor reap nor gather into barns, and yet your heavenly Father feeds them" (Mt 6:26). Jesus painted pictures with words, like the stained glass windows that adorn the majority of Christian churches. Mental images of biblical scenes are like painted prayers.

Ignatius Loyola took this a step farther by encouraging people to pray by putting themselves in gospel scenes. You may say, "Well I don't have much of an imagination." That's OK. Just having a sense of a scene suffices.

How to Let God Penetrate Your Imagination

One way to use the imagination in prayer is to pick a scene from the Gospels, preferably one that includes Jesus.

First, prepare yourself for the guided meditation. Before you begin this prayer exercise sit in a comfortable chair and relax. There are many ways to relax, to put yourself in a frame of mind to be able to enter fully into meditation. Some use the Jesus Prayer, for instance, as a way of letting God calm them. Imagining themselves in a favorite place, such as the seashore, calms others. Hear the waves rolling in, feel the wind, see Jesus meet you on the seashore and take your hand for a moment. Breathe deeply . . . relax.

> *In a whisper Jesus tells you, "I want you to know it is safe, so very safe, to be here with me.*

Now you are ready to begin the guided meditation. Read it at a snail's pace, scene by scene, sentence by sentence. As you read, pause, close your eyes a moment, and imagine the scene. Pause when you feel a grace or anointing on a particular scene or phrase. After you have finished reading

46

the guided prayer, line by line, close your eyes and as best
you can carry yourself through the whole scene without
referring to the book.

Place yourself in the scene, and imagine as vividly as possible
the sights, the feel, and the sounds.

The majority of the prayer journeys at the end of chapters
in this book contain guided meditations. The Scriptures for
prayerful reading given in the prayer exercises at the end of
each chapter will also help you to enter more fully into the
peacefulness.

Dear Lord, there are times that I grow weary,
Tired from so many worries and pains.
Empty me of my distresses,
for I give to you my tensions and my strains.
Lift me up on wings like an eagle's.
Fill me with your love, remove all stains.
For Lord you are near me,
Nearer than my own breathing and my own heartbeat.
Refresh me; revive me, like summer's cooling rains. Amen.

Prayer Journeys

A Prayerful Reading *(lectio divina)*

Read these passages slowly,
frequently pausing to listen for the still, small voice of God.

Every valley shall be lifted up,
and every mountain and hill be made low;
the uneven ground shall become level,
and the rough places a plain.
Have you not known? Have you not heard?
The LORD is the everlasting God,
the Creator of the ends of the earth.
He does not faint or grow weary;
his understanding is unsearchable.
He gives power to the faint,
and strengthens the powerless.
Even youths will faint and be weary,
and the young will fall exhausted;
but those who wait for the LORD shall renew their strength,
they shall mount up with wings like eagles,
they shall run and not be weary,
they shall walk and not faint.

(ISAIAH 40:4, 28–31).

A Guided Meditation: Sitting with Jesus

Close your eyes. Imagine another chair beside you.

In your mind's eye, you become aware Jesus entering the room. Imagine him in any way that feels comfortable to you.

Jesus sits in a chair beside you. He takes your hand in his. With your fingers, you can trace the nail print in his hand. Deep peace comes from him. His love warms your hand. The healing warmth flows up through your hand into your arm, warming you, healing you. That warmth now calms the muscles of your shoulder. The warmth of His love fills your chest and surrounds your heart.

Rest there a while, and be still and at peace in Jesus' presence.

Next, Jesus speaks to you quietly and tenderly. In a whisper He tells you, "I want you to know it is safe, so very safe, to be here with me. As you feel ready, one by one tell me some of the stresses and worries that weigh you down."

Tell Him about your stresses and worries.

Journal Time

Your life is an abundant source of scenes of comfort. Too often we forget those times. What are some scenes in your life that you find comforting, and why?

Jesus brought comfort to many. Which is your most comforting scene from the Gospels? Write a Guided Meditation in which you place yourself within that Gospel scene.

"Since then we have a great high priest, we must pass through the heavens, Jesus, the Son of God, let us hold fast to our confession. For we have not the high priest who is unable to sympathize with our weakness, but one who in every respect has been tempted as we are, yet without sin. Let us then with confidence draw near to the throne of grace, that we may receive mercy."

(HEBREWS 4:14–16)

5

Meeting God in Intimate Conversation

*"Always act toward God like faithful friends who consult
with each other on everything ... Accustom yourself
to speak to God, one-to-one, in a familiar manner as to the
dearest friend you have and who loves you best of all."*

ALPHONSUS DE LIGOURI

IN THE SPRING OF 2004, some unexpected news at a doctor's
visit interrupted my life. First, I developed a bad chest cold,
and drove to a walk-in health center for treatment. After
he listened to my chest, the doctor said it might be
pneumonia and immediately sent me to a nearby room for a
chest x-ray.

The results did suggest early pneumonia. Worse, the chest
film showed a large nodule on my lung as well as scarring. He
immediately arranged for a CT-scan the next day at a local
hospital.

I didn't worry. After all, I had never smoked, and I saw
myself as robust and healthy. Three days after the scan

when the doctor called with the results, I thought, *This will be good news.*

Instead his grim words quickly cut through my hopeful mood, "The CT report shows a nodule deep in your lung. The report reads, 'Must be considered carcinoma until proven otherwise.'" He referred me to a pulmonologist, a lung specialist.

The pulmonologist wanted a second opinion, and sent me for a CT at a different hospital. The second report confirmed the first: "Must be considered carcinoma unless proven otherwise."

Suddenly I faced the prospect of a long, draining illness. Lung surgery and chemotherapy loomed, treatments likely to make me feel sick and persistently nauseated. And despite the surgery and treatments, I would still likely die.

I had always thought I would take news of approaching death calmly. After all, as a Christian I believed death was not an ending, but a beginning: the start of everlasting life with our Lord Jesus. But instead of calm, a nearly overpowering sense of terror filled me.

> *Accustom yourself to speak to God, one-to-one, in a familiar manner as to the dearest friend you have and who loves you best of all.*
>
> ALPHONSUS DE LIGOURI

And yet, despite the CT results, my pulmonologist held out hope. He ran more tests to try to disprove the CT results. The other tests came out inconclusive. Finally, the pulmonologist referred me to the University of Alabama Medical College Hospital in Birmingham, where I met with a renowned chest surgeon.

The surgeon's first words were, "God bless you." Grave concern and compassion came through in his voice. He arranged for me to return the next Thursday for further tests, and put me on the surgery schedule for a lung resection and removal of the growth the day afterward.

That whole week before surgery, stress so tied me up that I found prayer impossible. However, toward the end of that week, through sheer will power I forced myself to open a conversation with God.

"Dear Jesus, I am scared and terrified."

It was all I could squeeze out. I talked to God simply repeating those same words, for fifteen or twenty minutes. It surely was not an eloquent prayer, but at least I wasn't holding back. The raw honesty of the prayer slowly quieted my soul.

As I grew still, other words followed. I said, "Lord I know you love me tenderly. You have walked at my side throughout my life. You have helped me through so many rough spots. Please ease my soul, and let me know what You hold in store for me as I go through this suffering." Just conversing with God deepened the calm. At least now I was not alone. I rested awhile in the tranquility of God's nearness. God's presence warmed me, as if He were whispering to me, "I love you with an everlasting love, I will never let go of you."

Spontaneously, one prayer following another overflowed from my heart. Praise and thanks poured out of me. "Lord Jesus, thank You for loving-kindness, Your splendor. I thank You that You became one of us, that You died for us, rose again for us, and will come to gather us to Your bosom."

Next, I began fervently to pray for others, keenly feeling their needs as I prayed for them. I prayed for peace and justice in the world. This intercessory prayer turned my thoughts away from myself to the cares of others. After talking with God for a while, a Bible verse came to mind, "I have loved you with an everlasting love; I have drawn you with loving-kindness" (Jer 31:3).

See the whole world surrounded and embraced by the light of Christ, which streams from His empty tomb.

Thursday at the Medical College, they used their advanced, state-of-the-art CT scan and PET scan to take yet more pictures of my lung. That afternoon I met with the chest surgeon again. This time I was calm, at peace, ready for whatever unfolded. The surgeon smiled broadly at me, saying, "You are going home today, there will be no surgery. Our equipment is more advanced than the equipment in Columbus. The CT film showed the lump is a fatty deposit, and the PET scan also suggested it was not cancer."

Silently, I thanked God for His mercies to me. I thanked Him for the wonderful friends and family He had given me, and for my ministry as a deacon. And I thanked Him for that wayward lump of fat.

Lord Jesus, You are more intimate to us than we are to ourselves.
You hear the rumblings of our heart,
You listen to us as none other.
You feel our emotions, observe our thoughts, watch our footsteps.
You speak to the bosom of our souls
You are so near, so present.
We acknowledge your closeness and thank you for your love, and for your splendor.
We ask you to help us Lord, especially when we grow weary with stress and worry.
Help us to pour our hearts out to you, to tell you of our worries, our sins and our pains.
Help our brothers and sisters in faith. We bring to you their needs and cares.
Pour out your healing love upon them. Amen.

Conversational Prayer:
An intimate communion with God that eases the soul

While the news about my medical condition was good this time, I knew it would not always be good. The news is never *always* good, not for any of us. And yet, through this experience I had learned that whatever bad news is in my future, I can talk to God and He can talk to me.

This assurance is at the heart of Conversational Prayer, an intimate communication between friends. Jesus listens to us; we listen to Him. Hardly anything comforts and eases us more that someone who lovingly listens. Jesus — the greatest listener, the greatest friend — experienced our fears, our stresses and worries. He understands us more than anyone.

Alphonsus de Liguori, the patron saint of Conversational Prayer, lived in Italy during the eighteenth century. In his book, *Prayer As Conversing with God as a Friend,* he wrote: *"God's heart has no greater concern than to love us and to make itself loved by us."* This is the core principle of Conversational Prayer. He continues, "Always act toward God like faithful friends who consult with each other on everything . . . Accustom yourself to speak to God, one-to-one, in a familiar manner as to the dearest friend you have and who loves you best of all."

Not only do we speak with God in Conversational Prayer, God speaks to us: "God will not make himself heard by you in a voice that reaches your ears but rather in a voice that only your heart knows well."

How to Start a Conversation with God

Any prayer in which you converse personally with God can be called "conversational prayer." Rosalind Rinker, a former Protestant missionary to China, has written a score of books on Conversational Prayer, and has led hundreds of experiential workshops on the subject. She worked closely with the Catholic bishop of Little Rock in teaching Conversational Prayer throughout his diocese. Her work influenced the widely used Catholic Bible study called the Little Rock Bible Study.

> *"God will not make himself heard by you in a voice that reaches your ears but rather in a voice that only your heart knows well."*
> *Alphonsus de Liguori*

Like Alphonsus, she defines Conversational Prayer as a form of "spontaneous, childlike prayer, put out from hearts directly to the heart of Jesus." As much as possible, she urges people to pray out loud as they converse with God. I have found speaking the words just under my breath, moving tongue and lips a little, physically reinforces the prayer and works just as well. (Some people write out their Conversational Prayers.)

The following steps of prayer were drawn from Rosalind Rinkers's four steps in conversational prayer.

Rosalind Rinker's Four steps of conversation prayer

Jesus is here. Recognize the Risen Lord's nearness. Welcome Him out loud or silently in your own words. I often pray: "You are so near me, Lord, closer to me than my breath. Please open Your listening heart to my prayers."

Thank You, Lord. Think over all the ways Jesus has loved and cared for you. Name some of those times, and thank Him for them. Offer praise, worship and adoration.

Help me, Lord. We take our needs to Jesus one by one. We tell Him about our cares, admit our sins, and ask Him for guidance.

I pray for my brothers and sisters. We move beyond ourselves to pray for others. We think of their needs, their cares. We pray for this hurting world of ours. We open our hearts wide in compassion.

PRAYER JOURNEYS

Prayerful Reading (*Lectio Divina*)

"Do not worry about anything, but in everything by prayer and supplication with thanksgiving let your requests be made known to God. And the peace of God, which surpasses all understanding, will guard your hearts and your minds in Christ Jesus."

(PHIL 4:6–7)

Because you have made the LORD your refuge,
the Most High your habitation, no evil shall befall you,
no scourge come near your tent.
For he will give his angels charge of you,
to guard you in all your ways.
On their hands they will bear you up,
lest you dash your foot against a stone.
You will tread on the lion and the adder,
the young lion and the serpent you will trample under foot.
Because he cleaves to me in love, I will deliver him;
I will protect him, because he knows my name.
When he calls to me, I will answer him;
I will be with him in trouble,
I will rescue him and honor him.
With long life I will satisfy him,
and show him my salvation.

(PSALM 91:9–16)

A Guided Meditation: *Light of the Risen Christ*

Take time to be still. Perhaps say the Jesus Prayer. Let the love of God pour over you. Rest in the calm awhile. You find yourself walking in along a rocky path in another place, another time.

It's early morning, twilight, just a moment before the sun rises. You turn a corner and come to a tomb with the stone rolled away. Light pours from the empty tomb. Suspended in air at the entrance of the tomb is Jesus, His face bright with joy. His arms are outstretched, and you can see the wounds the nails made in His hands and feet. You see the wound the spear made in His side. Brilliant light shines from each wound.

You stand still, looking at Jesus as He looks at you. The light that encircles Him now enfolds you. The light caresses you, nurtures you, and warms you, as it brings great joy. You breathe in the light. It fills your lungs. The light surrounds your blood cells until — inside and out — you are saturated with the light. This is the light of Christ, the light that remakes the world. That light now remakes you brings you to fresh life.

Rest a moment in the light. As you look at Jesus, talk to Him.

First thank Him. Thank Him for all the ways His love has helped you.

Next, tell Him your needs. Tell Him about the ways you need His help in your life.

Now tell Him about other people and situations that need His help. Pray for peace and justice. Pray that human life be respected and protected from the moment of conception till the moment of natural death. See the whole world surrounded and embraced by the light of Christ, which streams from His empty tomb.

Gently return to this time and rest in the stillness.

Journal Time

1. God writes a letter to you about how the resurrection can change your life. What do you think it says?

2. We are not saved alone, and we are not healed alone. We are healed and saved and healed together with brothers and sisters, together with the whole cosmos. Write a letter to God asking His help and intervention for different people in your life and situations in the world that concern you.

"When God forgives us,

he tosses our sins into the deepest

part of the ocean,

and then puts up a sign that says

'No Fishing.'"

CORRIE TEN BOOM

6

How Forgiveness
Can Lighten Your Load

"The sacrifice acceptable to God is a broken spirit;
a broken and contrite heart, O God,
you will not despise."
PSALM 51:17

EVA LAY TERRIFIED IN HER BED IN CARDIAC CARE ICU after a
massive heart attack. She was totally alone. It was not
something she had ever anticipated, yet here she was. Her
husband of forty years had died three years before. Their one
child, Billy, had died in a car accident twenty years earlier.
At the age of seventy, she was retired from her profession as
an attorney, and had no close friends. She hated the isolation
of living alone; it was almost too much for her to endure. Yet
she had no options.

Eva's one sibling, her younger sister Mary, lived in another
part of the city; but they barely spoke. The two sisters had
been close until Mary entered high school. Eva was the
studious one, making straight A's. Mary paid little attention to

her schoolwork, but paid lots of attention to boys, her social life, and the most stylish clothes. Mary had people skills, but not academic skills. In addition, their parents seemed to favor Mary. Despite her achievements, Eva felt left out, slighted. She resented all the attention Mary received.

Finally the two sisters experienced a stormy estrangement when they were in their late forties. When their widowed mother became too feeble to live alone, Eva took charge.

Max Lucado calls resentment the "cocaine of emotions." It revs people up. It energizes them. It numbs them from pain, and addicts them as surely as cocaine.

She arranged for their mother to get the finest care at an expensive assisted living facility, which Eva would pay for. Then Mary rushed in and offered to care for their mother in her own modest home, an offer their mother immediately accepted.

Eva boiled over with rage. She cornered her sister and stormed at her, "You know she'll get the best care in assisted living. You're not a responsible person, you've never been responsible. You are doing this just to collect mother's life insurance and her savings. As far as I am concerned, I no longer have a sister."

Mary responded with equally hard words.

During the two years their mother lived, Eva dutifully dropped by to visit her mother at Mary's every two weeks; but her manner was aloof and barely civil. After their mother's death, Eva dropped off all contact with Mary.

Yet each Christmas and on each of her birthday's Eva would get a card from Mary saying, "I love you and I'm praying for you." Mary was doing her best to keep up some contact with Eva.

Her second morning in ICU, Eva woke up and found a woman standing beside her with tears in her eyes. The face was familiar, but Eva just couldn't make it out. Then the woman's hand brushed her forehead and she whispered softly, "Eva I love you, I love you more than you can know."

It was Mary. Eva was not alone. Now, the troubles and resentments of decades washed away. They were simply two sisters who loved each other.

Mary remained by Eva's side every day; it was as though there had never been a breach in their relationship. When she was discharged from the hospital, Mary took Eva into her own home to recuperate. Mary's faith had deepened over the many years, and her forgiveness for her sister had deepened, too. That forgiveness had just needed the right time to manifest itself.

When We Resent, We Hurt Ourselves

When we don't forgive others that failure to forgive can turn into resentment, and few things wound like resentment. When we hold on to resentment, we are the ones who hurt.

Max Lucado calls resentment the "cocaine of emotions." It revs people up. It energizes them. It numbs them from pain, and addicts them as surely as cocaine.

Persistent resentment can become a false but all-consuming pleasure. People can come to enjoy their own resentment.

Resentment is about power and control. It is a drug that inebriates, and few things deliver the mighty rush of power that hurting others can deliver. And yet, resentment also rips us apart. It wrecks our relationships. When we resent, we no longer have time to breathe in the freshness of each moment. We cease to see the beauty in the world. Hatred leaves little room for love of any sort.

When we resent, we push away those who love us, even those who have never hurt us and never will. At times we can even push away God with our resentment. The first step in breaking this pattern and forgiving others is to realize how much God has forgiven us personally.

God is a lavish forgiver. Coming to Him often to be forgiven teaches us about how we should forgive others.

Why People Don't Seek Forgiveness

Sadly, the idea of going to God to be forgiven holds little popularity today, even in many churches. In today's society, it is much easier to blame others for our failings, to count all the ways we have been wronged and use those wrongs as excuses for our current failings.

In our own minds, if we are no longer responsible for our actions and our feelings, we need never seek forgiveness. Instead we say, "My past made me do this; the unfairness of the world has left me unable to take control of my life." A young man addicted to alcohol, instead of seeing his alcoholism as a disease and taking responsibility for his actions, might instead complain: "I can't help myself, my father didn't pay enough attention to me when I was little. He rarely came to my Little League games."

It is so easy for adult children to blame sins and failings on their parents or on other factors rather than to seek forgiveness and admit their own failings.

What is Forgiveness?

How often have you heard people say with clenched teeth, "I can forgive, but I can never forget." Forgiveness always involves at least some forgetting. We don't deny the hurt done to us, repress it, or minimize it. Instead, with God's help and the help of others, we grieve, let go, and move on. We no longer allow the hurt done to us, or the person who did the hurting, to control us.

When we resent, we push away those who love us, even those who have never hurt us and never will. At times we can even push away God with our resentment

Forgiveness is usually not instantaneous, it is a process, it takes time. Just wanting to start down the journey toward forgiveness is enough in God's eyes. God's forgiveness toward us is like a canceled banknote, burned and written off the books. That's what God's forgiveness is like. He forgets the wrong for all eternity.

Once I heard a story of a Filipino priest, a devout man who prayed frequently and was a healing force within his congregation. It seems that in seminary he committed a serious sin that was so bad in his mind, he had never told anyone about it outside the confessional.

In his parish there was a woman reputed to have visions of Jesus in her dreams. As was prudent, the priest was skeptical about her visionary claims. One day after weekday morning Mass, wanting to test the genuineness of her visions, he asked her if Jesus had appeared to her in her dreams the night before. When she said He had, the priest asked her, "The next time Jesus appears to you at night, ask Him to tell you what the sin was I committed in seminary."

> *"God pardons like a parent, who kisses the offense into everlasting forgetfulness"*
> – HENRY WARD BEECHER

He didn't see the woman for several days and when he finally saw her, he asked, "Has Jesus appeared to you again?"

She answered, "Yes."

"Did you ask him what sin I committed in seminary?" he continued.

"Yes."

"Well, what did he say?"

The woman answered, "He said, 'I forget.'"

That great evangelical preacher of the nineteenth century, Henry Ward Beecher said, "God pardons like a parent, who kisses the offense into everlasting forgetfulness. "

Even more, God's forgiveness does for the human heart

what sunshine does for a plant; it warms it and stimulates growth.

Take time each day to tell God about the shadows of your soul. If you are Catholic or Orthodox, you can complete and seal that forgiveness by frequenting the Sacrament of Reconciliation. And as we experience God's forgiveness, we will begin to forgive others in our life as freely as God forgives us.

Learning How to Love our Enemies

The next step is learning to bless the one you might now resent. Jesus says: "Love your enemies and pray for those who persecute you, so that you may be children of your Father in heaven..." (Mt 5:44).

Begin to pray for that person. Hard as it may be, begin to see that person as a child of God, just as you are. Imagine what that person's world is like. Think of the pain that person endured that led them to hurt instead of help. Begin the process of seeing the person as a struggling child of God, like you. "Know all and you will pardon all," Thomas A Kempis wrote in *The Imitation of Christ*, seven hundred years ago.

Dear Lord, Your forgiveness is the medicine that heals, the salve that calms, the touch that mends. Help me acknowledge candidly my sinfulness, ways that I have hurt you or others, ways that I have broken your commands. Help me to pour out to you any bitterness that I may harbor in my soul. I call upon your compassionate heart to help me forgive others as lavishly as you have forgiven me. Give me the wisdom on how to reconcile with others, when reconciliation is possible. Amen.

PRAYER JOURNEYS
A Prayerful Reading (*Lectio Divina*)

If I speak in the tongues of mortals and of angels,
but do not have love,
I am a noisy gong or a clanging cymbal.
And if I have prophetic powers,
and understand all mysteries and all knowledge,
and if I have all faith so as to remove mountains but
do not have love, I am nothing.
If I give away all my possessions,
and if I hand over my body to be burned,
but do not have love, I gain nothing.

Love is patient; love is kind;
love is not envious or boastful or arrogant or rude.
It does not insist on its own way;
it is not irritable or resentful;
it does not rejoice in wrongdoing,
but rejoices in the truth.
It bears all things, believes all things,
hopes all things, endures all things.

Love never ends. But as for prophecies,
they will come to an end;
as for tongues, they will cease; as for knowledge,
it will come to an end.
For we know only in part, and we prophesy only in part;

but when the complete comes,

the partial will come to an end.

When I was a child, I spoke like a child,

I thought like a child, I reasoned like a child;

when I became an adult, I put an end to childish ways.

For now we see in a mirror, dimly,

but then we will see face to face.

Now I know only in part; then I will know fully,

even as I have been fully known.

And now faith, hope, and love abide, these three;

and the greatest of these is love.

1 CORINTHIANS 13:1–13

A Guided Meditation: *Giving and Getting Forgiveness*

Part One: Seat yourself in a comfortable chair and take time to grow still. Perhaps repeat the Jesus Prayer. The love of God fills the room. You feel someone grasp your shoulders from behind. It is Jesus. Peace, calm, and assurance flow from His hands into you. You feel safe, so very safe.

Take time to remember the last time you experienced the release of forgiveness. Perhaps it was the relief and joy of experiencing the Sacrament of Reconciliation. Maybe it was a time someone in your life reached far inside their hearts and forgave you. Experience again the peace of that moment. Now Jesus moves from behind your chair to your front. He sits in a chair facing you. He takes your two hands in His. You know He wants you to search your heart for ways that you have hurt yourself, God, or others; for times that you have broken God's commandments. Tell Him about your sins and experience His tender compassion and forgiveness. If you are Catholic or Orthodox, complete this act of contrition by celebrating the Sacrament of Reconciliation.

Take time each day to tell God about the shadows in your soul.

Part Two: You are seated in a chair; behind you is Jesus, holding your shoulders. It is so very safe to be there with Jesus. In front of you is an empty seat.

Now picture someone you have been close to you, but who has hurt you deeply, step in and sit in that seat facing you. What feelings do you have? Remember Jesus is there, protecting and comforting you. His strong hands on your shoulder keep you calm.

Forgiveness is a process, not an instant event. Are you ready to begin the process of forgiveness with the person in front you? It's OK if you are not ready. Jesus can help you begin that process later in your life when you are ready.

If you think you are ready to begin, look into the person's eyes, and survey the face. What pain and difficulty in life do you think shaped them? Try to see the world from that person's perspective. You hear the person ask you, "What could I have done to love you better?"

Tell that person what they could have done to love you better. Only if you feel ready, tell them you are ready to begin the process of forgiving him or her. Only if you feel safe doing so, walk up to the person and clasp that person's hands in affection. Jesus comes and joins the two of you, placing a hand on your shoulder while placing a hand on the other person's shoulder.

Journal Time

1. Our God is in the forgiveness business! Describe some ways that you can daily open up yourself to the gift of God's forgiveness.

2. We celebrate God's forgiveness by forgiving others. Think of one person that needs your forgiveness. How can you bring that forgiveness about?

"Therefore I tell you, do not worry about your life, what you will eat or what you will drink, or about your body, what you will wear. Is not life more than food, and the body more than clothing? Look at the birds of the air; they neither sow nor reap nor gather into barns, and yet your heavenly Father feeds them. Are you not of more value than they?"

MATTHEW 6:25–26

CHAPTER

7

How to Let Go of Worry

Do not worry about anything,
but in everything by prayer and supplication
with thanksgiving let your requests be made known to God.
PHILIPPIANS 4:6

SEVERAL YEARS AGO I PREACHED A MISSION in a moderate size
parish in the Southwest. The attendance was high on the
first night. People listened with animated faces. And yet,
while the congregation seemed to enjoy the first talk, the
pastor sat up front, his face stern and emotionless.
Immediately I feared the worst. Surely something I said had
angered him.

After I finished the talk, the pastor came up to me and
said, "Tomorrow could you come by my office? I want to
discuss this talk with you."

Now I was certain that I had upset him and that he
would call me to task. My imagination ran wild with scene
after scene of possible grim outcomes. The pastor might call
my diocese and tell them I did a lousy job. His assessment

of my talk would pass throughout his diocese, and I would never receive an invitation to speak in that state again. Sleepless much of that night, I fought with the covers till nearly morning.

When I entered his office late the next morning, my heart pounded. Fear gripped me. But as I sat down, I noticed this time his face was full of expression. He smiled broadly. "The talk you gave was one the best I have ever heard on the subject of prayer. I was wondering, do you have a tape of that talk? If so, could we use it in our adult education program?"

> *"Worry can be a relentless scavenger, roaming the corners of your mind, feeding on anything, never leaving you alone."*
> EDWARD M. HALLOWELL

As it turned out, his emotionless face the night before had simply been the result of tiredness, and had nothing to do with me or the talk. My worries proved baseless, as worries often are. I had been doing what psychologists call "awfulizing" or "catastrophizing," blowing concerns out of proportion, making them far worse than they really are.

Worry—A Disease of the Imagination

In his book *Worry*, Harvard Medical School psychiatrist Edward M. Hallowell calls worry "a disease of the imagination." When fear and stress rise to the cerebral cortex, the mind imagines the worst possibilities. Our thoughts turn toxic, thinking of possible dire consequences.

When we worry, a slide show of terrible possibilities flows

through our minds. Worries come unbidden, lessening our enjoyment of work, our friends and family, and even God. Hallowell, a practicing Christian, suggests that *worry is a form of fear.* When fear reaches the cerebral cortex—the part of the brain that thinks and feels, remembers and imagines—thoughts and emotion are added to the fear, deepening its power. Worry leaves us with an intense sense of powerlessness and vulnerability.

Hallowell says that when worry is at its worst, "worry can be a relentless scavenger, roaming the corners of your mind, feeding on anything, never leaving you alone." When overcome by worry, Hallowell says, "Don't wring your hands, clasp them... Prayer or meditation can change the state of your brain... Talk to God when you feel worried."

"Toxic" Worry

Some worry is good for us. A student preparing for a test needs a degree of worry to motivate good study habits. A mother with an infant should have at least some worry to remind her to watch her child closely. However, worry turns toxic when it interferes with our daily functioning, preoccupies us, or drags us down.

Hallowell says one of the early meanings of the word worry was "to gnaw." A dog digs up a bone, shakes it, grinds it, growls with it in his mouth. In short, he "worries" the bone. While worrying the bone, the dog doesn't see the beauty of the afternoon sun. He is too preoccupied.

Just as the dog will not let go of the bone, a worried

person won't let go of the object of his or her concern, says Hallowell, "biting and chewing it into the quick of his life. Nipping and picking and looking for meat but only finding bones and remnants."

Prayer Breaks the Cycle of Worry

So, how can we break this cycle of "toxic" worry and begin to live a life of freedom and grace? When worries grow severely toxic, talking out your worries with a trained doctor or therapist is essential. Talking worries over with a trusted family member or friend can also help.

> *Generations have found prayer to be a huge antidote to worry. Prayer breaks the cycle of constantly digging up our worries and chewing on them over and over again.*

And yet, talking with God about our concerns is every bit as important if we truly want to gain a sense of peaceful perspective. Generations have found prayer to be a huge antidote to worry. Prayer breaks the cycle of constantly digging up our worries and chewing on them over and over again.

John, a family physician, faced a difficult problem: His wife, June, suffered from alcoholism—yet she refused to recognize her disease. At times she would lash out at their two daughters, aged nine and ten, calling them lazy, worthless, not fit to be her daughters. Then an hour or two after her tirades, she turned into the picture of a loving mother doting on her children. Her moods swung swiftly. At times when she was supposed to be watching the girls, she lay sprawled out on her bed instead. Once when she lay passed out on the bed, the younger daughter started a kitchen fire while attempting to cook lunch.

John himself experienced both her hostility and her loving side. However, her changes in mood left him constantly drained and on guard. John felt abandoned and alone in dealing with his wife's problems. He seemed to have no one to whom he could turn.

He had always thought of their first twelve years of marriage as wonderful. Before the alcohol took over, he thought June was the best wife anyone could hope for. They had lived their lives in close harmony. But now, worry about his wife and the future of his family gripped him in the stomach both day and night.

Scenarios of dire outcomes passed before him. Would his wife's neglect of the children result in their injury? After all, the kitchen fire was a close call. He worried that his wife's verbal abuse of the two girls would permanently scar them. These worries caused sleepless nights and wore him out to the point he seemed lethargic. He also had to cope with a growing anger at his wife for her behavior. Drained of energy by his worries and anger, he found it difficult to be fully alert while seeing patients. He worried about accidentally making medical mistakes in his practice because of his condition.

His options seemed few. Divorcing his wife would be near impossible for him; he believed in the sanctity of marriage. Moreover, he could not be certain he would be awarded custody of the children. Any time he mentioned treatment, June raged and denied that she even had an alcohol problem. John's worries left him so beat down, he found it nearly impossible to take any action at all to resolve the family's problems. No matter how hard he pleaded, June would not even consider treatment.

In desperation, John approached one of his parish's deacons for help. The deacon, a caring listener, just encouraged John to unload his worries. After John finished, the deacon said in a soft tone, "You need to begin taking care of yourself. Cut your hours at work. Take time for long walks, for going fishing with your buddies. Most of all pray, read Scripture, and come to daily Mass when possible."

Then the deacon prayed with him, gave him a blessing, and closed by reading the following Scripture, "Peace I leave with you; my peace I give to you. I do not give to you as the world gives. Do not let your hearts be troubled, and do not let them be afraid" (John 14:27).

John memorized that Bible verse and repeated it slowly and silently throughout his day. He arrived at his office early to pray and read Scripture. Daily he unburdened himself to God in his prayer, pouring out his worries and anger. He made a special point of praying for his wife and her recovery every day. As he did this, his anger at his wife dissipated, replaced by compassion and tenderness. He realized that his wife's addiction to alcohol must be terrible for her. He imagined her loneliness, her fear of being held in the grip of a disease she could not control. His worries lost some of their crippling force.

Then everything turned worse. In deep winter, June and their ten-year-old daughter drove around town, running errands. Not in control of herself, June left her daughter in the car as she went into a bar. "One small drink would not hurt," June thought. "I'll be finished in there in just a minute."

The minute turned in to an hour. One drink turned into three. When June returned to her car, she found her daughter shaking all over because of the cold. She saw the beginnings of frostbite on her daughter's face. Panicked, she called John and honestly told him what happened and asked him to rush over. She embraced her daughter, saying repeatedly, "I'm so sorry, sweetheart, at what I've done to you."

When John arrived, he moved his frightened daughter to his car and quickly drove to the emergency room. After examining her, the doctor assured John that there would be no permanent physical scarring, and sent the father and daughter home with prescriptions of different lotions to use on her face. They found June at home, curled on the bed in a fetal position, with her fists tightened up.

Before he began seeing the deacon and praying daily for his wife, John's anger might have overpowered him, causing

He knows that you are carrying many stresses and worries. And he says to you, "Let me help you with your anxiety."

him to severely chastise his wife. Now his heart opened wide with compassion and devotion to her. He walked over to the bed, lay down beside his wife, tenderly embracing her, and in a voice choked with tears said, "I love you June, more than I can ever express. I will always love you, be sure of that. Until the disease took over you were the brightness in my life; and you will be again. It's time June, its time to get treatment."

She whispered back to him, "I know dear, it's time."

The next morning she entered rehabilitation, and has now been sober for two years. Like all alcoholics, she will always be in recovery, but now she has help.

Dear Lord, you made us to be close to you, near you. You have linked our heart with yours. You know how to calm us as no one else can. Your very touch can lighten our loads.

It is so easy, Lord, to be overcome with worry, so easy for a problem to gnaw at us as a dog gnaws on a bone. Only your intervention can break the cycle of worry, the cycle of stress.

Today please help us to remember our worries, one by one, and to entrust each of them to you. It is so easy to worry about the past, the present and the future, so easy for imaginations to run wild with thoughts of dire consequences. Come to us now, Lord Jesus, lift up our hearts and bring us your peace. Empty us of worry and fear, then fill us with your presence. Amen.

PRAYER JOURNEYS
A Prayerful Reading (*Lectio Divina*)

Therefore I tell you, do not worry about your life,
what you will eat or what you will drink,
or about your body, what you will wear.
Is not life more than food,
  and the body more than clothing?
Look at the birds of the air;
they neither sow nor reap nor gather into barns,
and yet your heavenly Father feeds them.
Are you not of more value than they?
And can any of you by worrying add a single hour
  to your span of life?
And why do you worry about clothing?
 Consider the lilies of the field,
how they grow; they neither toil nor spin,
  yet I tell you,
  even Solomon in all his glory was not clothed
  like one of these.
  But if God so clothes the grass of the field,
which is alive today and tomorrow is thrown into the oven,
will he not much more clothe you—you of little faith?
Therefore do not worry, saying, 'What will we eat?'
or 'What will we drink?' or 'What will we wear?'
For it is the Gentiles who strive for all these things;
and indeed your heavenly Father knows that you need
  all these things.

But strive first for the kingdom of God and his righteousness,
and all these things will be given to you as well.
So do not worry about tomorrow,
for tomorrow will bring worries of its own.
Today's trouble is enough for today.

MATTHEW 6:25–34,

A Guided Meditation: *Touch of Comfort*

You are seated in a chair. Directly in front of you is Jesus. He has come to comfort you. His presence brings a deep calm. He has come as your friend and as your Savior.

He knows that you are carrying many stresses and worries. And he says to you, "Let me help you with your anxiety." As He says this, a wonderful light surrounds the two of you. It is the light of Christ omnipresent. You breathe in the light, you take it into your lungs. It warms you, it comforts you.

Christ extends both arms, palms facing upward. You know what He wants you to do: He wants you to place your palms over His, so that your palms are touching. You feel the tender love of Jesus flow from His hands into yours.

He wants you to allow all the stresses, tensions and worries inside you to pass through you, out through the palms of your hands into His hands. You feel the flow of your stresses and worries just flow out of you into Jesus' palms. You feel a great experience of lightness because Jesus has been here to help you.

Journal Time

Worries can consume us. We need to bring them to the light that they may be lightened. Write a letter to God, telling Him about your worries.

If God wrote a letter to you about your worries, what do you think He would say?

"For a great many of us, the only notion that we have of prayer is asking God to give us something that we want. But there is a far higher region of communion than that, in which the soul seeks and finds, and sits and gazes, and aspiring possesses, and possessing aspires. Where there is no spoken petition for anything affecting outward life, there may be the prayer of contemplation such as the burning Seraphs before the Throne do ever glow with. The prayer of silent submission, in which the will bows itself before God; the prayer of quiet trust, in which we do not so much seek as cleave; the prayer of still fruition."

ALEXANDER MACLAREN

8

How to Release Worries
From the Past

"It is in vain that you rise up early and go late to rest, eating the bread of anxious toil; for he gives to his beloved in sleep."

PSALM 127:3

TOM WORRIED CONSTANTLY. If the phone rang, he was afraid that his wife or children might have been killed in an accident, or that the IRS was auditing him. Despite his worries, by most standards he had a strong marriage. His wife reaffirmed him often. He could feel her love, some of the time at least, but the thought still plagued him, "Does she truly care about me?" He also doubted his other close relationships.

When Tom first talked to me after I finished a talk at his parish, he poured out his worries – fear of a flu pandemic, fear of a possible recession that would cause him to lose his job, fear that his loved ones would grow sick and die. He wanted me to tell him that everything would be OK. Yet no amount of reassurance calmed him.

I was so concerned I asked him to meet me at the church office in two days for another session. When we talked, I asked him to tell me about his past. Emotion left him and his voice turned flat when he talked about his childhood. He painted a favorable picture of his father. According to Tom, his father had been constantly attentive, involved with his burgeoning successes in Little League; in short, a father both strong and tender. Yet as he talked, I was sure he was leaving something out.

> *There is a child within us, the child we once were. The child within us carries the hurts of childhood. And while we can't remake the past, we can bring Jesus into the past.*

Finally, he told me the missing piece. Though his father held an executive job at which he performed well and genuinely worked hard at being a good father most of the time, Tom had a secret. His father would occasionally succumb to paranoid delusions. Today we would call this a delusional disorder, a mental disorder that is likely biochemically based. Most of the time, his father functioned well. But during episodes, the delusions would take him over and he would become a danger to himself and others. And since his mother withdrew and became passive during the crises, it fell to Tom as the oldest to handle the situations.

At age thirteen Tom and the whole family took a fun-filled vacation at the lake, where his father had been the model of paternal care. Sadly though, within days of returning home, his father lapsed into another episode: He claimed Tom, his wife, and the three younger siblings were plotting to kill him. He got his gun out and carried it in his belt around the house.

Tom's mother became so frightened she dealt with the problem as she usually did; she went to bed, rolled the pillow over her head, and withdrew. Once more, Tom had to handle this crisis. Terrified, he knew his first task was to calm his father. In a soft, comforting voice, he talked to his father and at last persuaded him to store the gun.

Next, he called his aunt and uncle, who lived nearby, for help. They immediately came over and took the whole family, except his father, to their grandmother's. His aunt and uncle then returned to the house, and after several hours persuaded Tom's father to seek help at the hospital.

Tom told me this story without emotion, betraying none of the terror he must have felt. The root of Tom's continuous worrying in the present was based on his sorrows from the past.

> *The children we once were are still within us. We can pray for our pasts as well as our present and our future.*

Worry: The Wounded Child Within Us

Sometimes when we worry constantly, it means we have failed to experience and face a sorrow that we felt at an earlier period in our lives. Worry becomes a defense against feeling past loss.

There is a child within us, the child we once were. The

child within us carries the hurts of childhood. And while we can't remake the past, we can bring Jesus into the past.

I knew Tom would get better as he slowly began to open his heart and grieve his lost childhood, allowing Christ's calm to surround the child he once was.

> *As you sit in your chair, imagine Jesus seated in front of you. You feel the peace and comfort that comes from His presence.*

Tom's inability to feel secure in his wife's love — and the love of those closest to him — was also rooted in the past. As a child he had seen that, no matter how good life was, it could all be shattered by one of his father's episodes. So, it's not unusual that Tom found it hard to trust his relationships and the successes of his life.

The children we once were are still within us. We can pray for our pasts as well as our present and our future.

Dear Jesus, you walked beside us when we did not even know you were there. You were with us when life bruised us and wore us down. You see how strains from the past are such a powerful, often hidden influence on the present.

Dear Lord, we open up to you pages of our past. Heal the little children we once were. Soothe the hurts that have accompanied us for a lifetime. Heal the scars. Help us to let go of all harmful worry, whether from the past or the present. For you are indeed, the healer, the comforter and restorer of our souls. Amen.

PRAYER JOURNEYS

We know that in everything God works for good
with those who love him, who are called according to his
purpose...
What then shall we say to this?

If God is for us, who is against us?
He who did not spare his own Son but gave him up for us all,
will he not also give us all things with him?

Who shall bring any charge against God's elect?
It is God who justifies; who is to condemn?
Is it Christ Jesus who died,
yes, who was raised from the dead,
who is at the right hand of God,
who indeed intercedes for us?

Who shall separate us from the love of Christ?
Shall tribulation, or distress, or persecution,
or famine, or nakedness, or peril, or sword?

As it is written,

"For thy sake we are being killed all the day long;
we are regarded as sheep to be slaughtered."
No, in all these things we are more than conquerors
through him who loved us.

For I am sure that neither death, nor life,
nor angels, nor principalities,
nor things present, nor things to come,
nor powers, nor height, nor depth,
nor anything else in all creation,
will be able to separate us from the love of God
in Christ Jesus our Lord.

(ROMANS 8:28, 31–39, RSV)

A Guided Meditation: *Calming the Child Within You*

Seat yourself comfortably and close your eyes. Say the Jesus Prayer awhile. Let the peace of Jesus grow deeply within you. You are in a park. It is a beautiful day, so relaxing, not a cloud in the sky. The sky is a brilliant blue. You view huge carpets of beautiful green grass wherever you look. You see the squirrels scurrying up and down trees, so peaceful, so relaxing.

You hear footsteps behind you. You turn your head, and there is Jesus. Picture him in any way that is comforting to you. Jesus stands beside you, and the two of you walk further down the pathway. You come to a park bench, and seated there is the grade school child you once were.

Jesus sits on one side of the child, and you sit on the other side.

What does it feel like to see yourself at this age? Quietly you tell the child who you are, that you are the adult self and that there is no need to be afraid. Introduce Jesus to the child. You look at the child to see if there is any stress, worry or pain in the child's body language or face.

Now put your arm around that child's shoulder. Introduce the child to Jesus; tell him or her that Jesus is someone who is safe; someone who loves without measure. Jesus puts His arms around the child, too. Jesus places His hands on the child's head and prays for the child. Then Jesus removes His hands, and you put your hands on the child's head. You pray for the child in your own words, as you let your hands rest there on the child's head.

Now it's time for you to part with your child. As you leave, assure the child that you and Jesus will always be there to protect him or her.

Open your eyes. Did any stress or worry from your childhood emerge while you were praying for the child? If so, tell Jesus about that stress and worry, and let His presence calm you. You can repeat this prayer exercise again and again, if you choose meeting the child you once were in infancy, as a middle schooler, or in high school.

A Guided Prayer Experience: A *Safe Place*

Part One. As you sit in a chair, imagine a place from your childhood where you felt protected and at peace, a place of safety. Perhaps it was your grandmother's house or a stream you liked to play in. Perhaps that place was your mother's lap. Vividly remember that place. Put yourself into the scene. Remember the safety, the sense of security. You feel a hand on your shoulder. It is Jesus standing behind you. He says to you, "You have a place of safety now in your life. I am that place of safety. Stay near me and I will keep you in peace."

Part Two. As you sit in your chair, imagine Jesus seated in front of you. You feel the peace and comfort that comes from His presence. In His lap is a photo album with images from your past that were full of stress and worry. He gently hands the book over to you. You look at those scenes. Now Jesus says to you, "Tell me the story behind one of those scenes of stress."

You tell him the story of that time of stress. When you finish, you sense His great love for you. He takes your hand in His, and you can feel comfort and love flow from His hands to yours, radiating through your whole body. You rest a moment in the peace. It is such a relief to tell that story to someone with such a compassionate heart. There is a wonderful light on Jesus' face, and that light now surrounds you, soothing you.

From God's point of view, even the most hurtful stories of our lives can contain seeds of strength and redemption. Take a moment and think of what God's perspective on your story might be.

Journal Time

1. Write a letter to the child you once were. (You can actually write several letters to children you once were at different ages. You can write a letter to the child you once were as a toddler, or in grade school or as a teen, for instance.) Reassure the child within you of Christ's love and your love. Comfort the child in the letter.

2. God was with us in our past, whether we recognized Him or not, caring and loving. Whatever wounds you, He feels too. If God were to write a letter to you to help heal the wounds of the past, what do you think He would say?

"Can a woman forget her
nursing child,
or show no compassion for the
child of her womb?
Even these may forget,
yet I will not forget you.
See, I have inscribed you on
the palms of my hands."

ISAIAH 49:15–16

9

The Stress-Relieving Power of Asking God's Help

"Go first to God; and when before Him pour out your whole heart, and you shall find that calm and stillness of heart.... If you do not find it all at once, pray on."

CANON MILLER

CAROLYN ACHIEVED MORE THAN ANYONE had expected. At twenty she had successfully completed the first two quarters of training at a nearby tech school toward becoming a teacher's assistant, a startling feat to all who loved her. There was a time this particular accomplishment wouldn't have been so remarkable. At seventeen she had excelled at academics; her eyes had shined with eagerness for life. Except for two or three B pluses over the years, she brought home a report card filled with A's. She was popular, too: vice president of her senior class. Active in her Methodist church, she read Scripture and prayed daily. She also helped lead retreats for her youth group.

Then, like a thunderclap, her life was forever altered.

Clambering up a tree with some of her cousins, she lost her balance and fell, hitting her head on a rock. Her terrified cousins couldn't wake her, sprawled out unconscious on the grass. Soon, paramedics rushed her to a nearby hospital emergency room. After several hours, she slowly awakened from her coma. Though groggy she appeared otherwise normal. The doctors held out hope for a full recovery.

> *The best way to handle our troubles, great or small, is spreading them before the Lord. Whatever is important enough to bother me, is important enough for me to speak to God about.*

Soon, however, events dashed that hope. Several days after returning home, she fell unconscious on the carpet in the grips of an uncontrolled epileptic seizure. Her doctor sent her to a neuro-psychologist to assess her brain functioning. A battery of tests showed brain damage. Her verbal functioning stayed high, but her visual-spatial abilities had been affected. Despite the 135 score on her verbal IQ, the injury had significantly impaired her overall memory, especially short-term memory. This created a dilemma for her. To the world she seemed bright and well spoken, but she now found it difficult to remember names and instructions, or what she had just read.

Carolyn finished high school, but not without much effort. Marshaling her courage, she registered in a teacher assistant program at her local tech school. However her memory problem made studying difficult — she had to read over her textbooks and listen to recordings from class lectures almost every waking moment. Her disability made it impossible for her to take notes. She asked the administration for a note taker as a way of accommodating her disability. (This was before the Americans With Disabilities Act had been in force.) The dean rebuffed her harshly. "What makes you think you are so special?" She tried to explain her condition to him, but before she finished, he interrupted her. "How can anyone as articulate as you have a disability?"

Carolyn swallowed hard and asked if she could use a cassette recorder in class. The dean replied gruffly, "Depends on if you can convince your teachers to let you."

Reluctantly, her first- and second-quarter teachers let her use her recorder. Several of her teachers, as well as some fellow students, simply thought she was seeking special privileges. Her ability with words masked her poor memory. During her third quarter, two teachers refused to allow her to use the recorder in class. Without the recorder or notes, she had no way of studying for the tests.

Despite holding a steady B average, Carolyn went about her day gripped by stress and worry. Tired out with constant studying, her devotional times ceased. She just didn't have the energy, she told herself. The school became hostile territory for her. She felt the school — teachers and students alike — didn't want her there. Getting an associate's degree as a teacher's assistant had seemed the only way for her to attain a measure of independence, and now that hope was being severely challenged. She felt trapped.

Frightened and nearly paralyzed with worry, Carolyn knew she needed help. So she made an appointment with her pastor. A caring listener, he let her pour out her stresses and frustrations. When she finished talking, she felt deeply relieved. "I wish I could have you by my side to listen twenty-four hours a day," Carolyn told him. "But I know that's not possible."

The pastor said, "Carolyn, there is someone who can listen to your distresses any time ... God." He then opened his Bible and read, "Do not worry about anything, but in everything by prayer and supplication with thanksgiving let your requests be made known to God. And the peace of God, which surpasses all understanding, will guard your hearts and your minds in Christ Jesus" (Philippians 4:6–7).

Our prayers become powerful when we turn the daily things we worry about into prayer.

The pastor explained that God yearns to hear our worries and anxieties, even the smallest ones. "Cast all your anxiety on him, because he cares for you" (1 Peter 5:7), the pastor urged Carolyn. Then he turned to the Book of Isaiah and read: "When you pass through the waters, I will be with you: and through the rivers, they shall not overflow you. When you walk through the fire, you shall not be burned, nor shall the flame scorch you" (Isaiah 43:2).

He printed out both of these Scriptures for her and asked

her to carry them around with her, and to read them slowly any time fear and uncertainty weighed her down. "As soon as you feel distresses, large or small, take them to God in prayer," the pastor said. "The best way to handle our troubles, great or small, is spreading them before the Lord. Whatever is important enough to bother me, is important enough for me to speak to God about." A shared confidence with a dear trusted friend has a soothing effect like few other things do. We feel safe, understood, cared for. This is especially true when God is that friend.

Carolyn followed her pastor's advice, daily talking over her problems and anxieties with God. Again and again she read those comforting Scriptures, and as she prayed she felt God take hold of her heart, bringing her tranquility. Finally she became clear-headed enough to realize that, unless she was able to record those two classes that didn't allow tape recorders, she had no way of passing. So she withdrew from school before she made any bad grades, and enrolled in another nearby college that had a program to help students with disabilities. The administration provided note-takers, and sent a letter to her teachers suggesting ways they might accommodate Carolyn.

Her spirits soared, and Carolyn's grades rose from B's to A's. In four years she graduated with a degree in elementary education, and now she teaches sixth grade at a nearby school. She still reads Scripture daily, and continues to pour out her needs and frustrations to God. In addition, she talks with her pastor at least once a month.

Our prayers become powerful when we turn the daily things we worry about into prayer. A low whisper of prayer to God can cause an avalanche of freshness and power within our lives. In the midst of our inner storms, we can throw the weight of cares upon God, and trust wholly in His help.

Come to God with Your Distresses

Just talking our problems over with God eases that worry.

Christian literature is filled with accounts of stressed-out people who came to God and found comfort and relief. Deep troubles tossed their lives this way and that, but when they finally took their problems to God, they found assistance.

As we go through the day with worry, anxiety, stress, and tension, swirling around us, we need to set aside time to articulate these distresses to God. When we do, often these problems no longer seem as big as we once thought. Just talking them over with God eases that worry.

Lord,

Your abundance fills the universe.

Your love can fill the crevices of my soul.

You know each of my steps, my coming and my going.

You know me thoroughly.

It is so easy for me to keep my needs hidden from not only myself but from you.

Like a parent you want me to tell you my needs,

Tell you of my sorrows.

Spread them out before you.

And you have promised me that when I bring them to you,

You will respond with tenderness, comfort and love.

I pause now to tell you my needs, one by one…

Prayer Journeys
A Prayerful Reading (*Lectio Divina*)

The LORD upholds all who are falling,
and raises up all who are bowed down.
The eyes of all look to thee,
and thou givest them their food in due season.
Thou openest thy hand,
thou satisfiest the desire of every living thing.
The LORD is just in all his ways. (RSV)

PSALM 145:14–17

A Guided Meditation: *Releasing Stones of Anxiety*

Settle yourself comfortably and close your eyes. It is a day full of God's beauty, but it is hard for you to appreciate the scenery: You are carrying a gunnysack filled with stones. You are climbing a mountain with the gunnysack slung over your shoulder.

It weighs you down. You are sweating.

All you can think about is your aching back.

Each of those stones represents a worry or stress in your life. There is no way you can let the gunnysack down.

You reach a grassy clearing, and you hear the grass rustle behind you. It is Jesus. He touches your shoulder with His hands, and His loving touch warms you, body and soul. Your spirit grows quiet, as it always does when Jesus is near.

"I've come to take your burdens," Jesus tells you kindly and quietly. "Give each one to me." So you reach in the gunnysack, and notice that He has a gunnysack as well. You pull out a rock; each rock in your sack is a specific worry or stress in your life. Perhaps it's a relationship worry, or a financial predicament. Whatever it is, tell Him what the worry is about and hand Him the stone. Do that with each stone in the gunnysack. As you hand Him each stone, He takes it from you and puts it in His gunnysack, until the sack He is carrying is filled with your stones.

You feel so much quieter. Your body is at rest. Your soul is at rest. You have handed over your burdens. You know that after Jesus fills up His gunnysack, the stones disappear. And you ask Jesus, how is it that the stones disappear?

"Because of Calvary," He answers simply. Thank Jesus in your own words for taking your burdens. Now you know what you can do with your burdens when they become heavy.

Journal Time

What is it you need? Write a prayer telling God your need and asking his help.

"When you have received some happy news, don't act like some local... people who run to God in times of difficulty but forget to adore Him when things are going well. You should be faithful to God as you would be to a friend who loves you and rejoices in your good fortune. Go to God and share your happiness with Him, give Him Praise and thanks, recognizing everything as a gift from His hands."

ALPHONSUS DE LIGUORI

10

How Thankfulness
Chases Away Worry

*"He who brings thanksgiving as his sacrifice
honors me;
to him who orders his way aright
I will show the salvation of God!"*
PSALM 50:23

THIRTY YEARS AGO, WHILE I WAS VISITING A MONASTERY in
the Midwest, I met a thirty-year-old man who lived there as
a lay associate. One evening I joined him while he was
preparing some newly felled logs for an addition to the
monastery. In a most unself-conscious way, he hummed
happily as he worked. Then, almost as if I were not there, he
began to pray softly as he trimmed a piece of a log: "I thank
you, Lord, for such a fine piece of wood. I thank you, Lord,
that it didn't rain and we had such a gorgeous sunlit day. I
thank you, Lord, that I have a place to lay my head and
companions that help me along the way."

Prayers of thanks poured out of him, and as he prayed a

brightness shone from his eyes. In the eyes of the world, he seemed as though he had little to be thankful for.

Alcoholism had destroyed his marriage, and although he was now in recovery he had lost custody of his two little girls. He was not even allowed by the courts to visit them. He knew he couldn't risk the environment at a normal job, for fear he would resume drinking. So he found surroundings much more conducive to sobriety — a monastery, where he worked for only room and board.

> *Giving thanks relieves our worry and stress by turning our thoughts from just ourselves to God's goodness.*

There was so much in his life that could have stressed him: not being able to see his children, not having what the world counts as regular employment. Despite this, his main mood was thankfulness and joy. Thankfulness chased away distress and worry. It can do the same for us, too.

Everything is a Gift From His Hands

If you are feeling stressed, get pen and paper out and begin a prayer of thanks. Start with the phrase, "I thank you, Lord, for …" Next write out, item by item, all the people and things for which you are thankful. Next, unhurriedly and prayerfully read what you have written. If a phrase strikes you, or "takes on anointing," just repeat that over and over again and let that carry you into the stillness.

As we enter wholeheartedly into this exercise each day, it

begins to form a habit of gratitude that will cause a change in our lives that Walter Brueggemann calls a shift from "disorientation to a new orientation." In this new orientation we are astounded by the love of God, by the intervention of God, by the surprising touch of God's comfort on our hearts. Such a movement "includes a rush of positive responses, including delight, amazement, wonder, awe, gratitude, and thanksgiving."

As we learn to appreciate life, we discover that blessings surround us even in the bleakest of times. Giving thanks relieves our worry and stress by turning our thoughts from just ourselves to God's goodness. Think of the last week in your life. What acts of kindness were done toward you? Focus on a person that you know loves you, someone with whom you have a current good relationship. See the beauty of that person in your mind's eye. Be thankful to God that you have someone like that in your life. Think of some of the ways God has touched you lately, and give thanks.

Thank you, Lord, for the beauty of this earth.
Thank you for the cosmos, and the immensity of its
splendor and light.
Most of all, thank you for sending your Son.
Through him, through his dying and rising,
you are remaking all creation.
And I thank you, Lord, that you are also remaking me.
You heal me, comfort me, console me, point me in new
directions.

My heart bursts with gratitude for your love.
A love full of majesty and vaster than the universe,
yet a love so warm, so close, so tender.
Thank you for the little blessings each day,
the people you have sent me,
and the ways you surprise me with your presence.
Help me to walk out into the world each day with gratitude on my face,
and thanksgiving in my heart.

As we learn to appreciate life, we discover that blessings surround us even in the bleakest of times

PRAYER JOURNEYS

A Prayerful Reading (Lectio Divina)

If the LORD had not been my help,
*   my soul would soon have dwelt in the land of silence.*
When I thought, "My foot slips,"
*   thy steadfast love, O LORD, held me up.*
When the cares of my heart are many,
*   thy consolations cheer my soul.* (RSV)

PSALM 94:17–19

O come, let us sing to the LORD;
*   let us make a joyful noise to the rock of our salvation!*
Let us come into his presence with thanksgiving;
*   let us make a joyful noise to him with songs of praise!*
For the LORD is a great God, and a great King above all gods.
In his hand are the depths of the earth;
*   the heights of the mountains are his also.*
The sea is his, for he made it; for his hands formed the dry land.
O come, let us worship and bow down,
*   let us kneel before the LORD, our Maker!*
For he is our God, and we are the people of his pasture,
*   and the sheep of his hand.*
O that today you would hearken to his voice!

PSALM 95:1–7

A Guided Meditation: *The Photo Album*

Find a quiet place and allow yourself to grow still. Perhaps repeat the Jesus Prayer awhile. After the silence settles over you, imagine that Jesus is seated in front of you. The light that surrounds him now surrounds you, calming you, helping you feel so peaceful.

Jesus is holding a picture album that contains pictures of happy and good times of your life. Look at the pictures of those graced times. See the person you once were in those pictures. Who else is in those happy pictures with you?

As you look over the pictures, gratitude begins to well up in your heart. Thank Jesus for each scene you see. Now, remember times in your life when you felt the closeness of God. Remember those times as vividly as you can. Thank Jesus for those times.

Sometimes when we remember the joyful times, we remember losses. Maybe those who were with us at those joyful times are no longer with us. Maybe relationships that were once full of happiness now have grown cold. If any distressful thoughts come to mind, tell Jesus about those thoughts and let him calm you.

Journal Time

Complete the following sentence, "I thank you, God,
for_____

2. Just as we appreciate what God has done for us, God appreciates *us*. Whenever we reach out to love our fellow human beings, God is touched. Whenever we turn to God, His heart is moved. If God were to write you a letter of appreciation for all the ways you have loved Him and loved others, what do you think the letter would say?

Peace I leave with you;
my peace I give to you.
I do not give to you as the
world gives.
Do not let your hearts be
troubled,
and do not let them be
afraid.

JOHN 14:27

CHAPTER

11

Finding The Peace
That Passes Understanding

"Thou dost keep him in perfect peace,
whose mind is stayed on thee…"
ISAIAH 26:3 (RSV)

WHEN I WAS SIX, I DREAMED OF BECOMING A PREACHER. Bible
in hand, I even practiced giving sermons to the cats in my
backyard. As I grew older the dream did not fade—and yet, a
mysterious difficulty held me back.

All throughout my childhood and early adulthood, I
found it difficult to complete simply visual-spatial tasks such
as dressing, brushing my teeth, or keeping my desk straight.
Though I yearned to play baseball, football and basketball, I
found those games bewildering. My handwriting was always
the worst in my class. It was particularly difficult for me in
junior high school, when other students laughed at my
difficulties.

My undiagnosed disability kept me constantly in trouble.
Some teachers angrily bore down on me for my illegible

papers and messy desk. One teacher said angrily, "You'll never amount to anything." Kinder teachers said that I had so much ability that I should apply myself and stop being so lazy.

Despite all this, I excelled in verbal skills. In the fifth grade, I had the vocabulary of a senior in high school. I read four grade levels above my own, and was seen toting around huge tomes such as *The Rise and Fall of the Roman Empire*.

Some people said I had a near photographic memory. And yet I took the sharp barbs of my teachers to heart, and berated myself for being so lazy, unmotivated, and confused. I chalked it up to a personal character flaw.

> *Our minds can't understand God's peace any more than the eye can hear an orchestra or the ear view a beautiful sunset. The sweetness of His peace, like eternity itself, can be felt, and touched, but never comprehended.*

Despite all this, at times an unexpected peace washed over me as though God was telling me that everything would be all right. With the support of understanding professors and my fellow students, I finished college. I continued on and attended Protestant seminary. However, my mysterious difficulties kept me from finishing.

When I was twenty-four, just after I became Catholic, my undiagnosed disability worsened. While crossing a road in rural Louisiana, a piece of farm equipment struck me. I landed on my head and was knocked unconscious. I spent a week in a rural hospital, but the doctor didn't run the appropriate tests to see if brain damage had resulted from the injury since I was so articulate.

In the weeks and months after the accident, I noticed my visual-spatial difficulties increase. Worse, I seemed to have lost much of my exceptional memory. My life continued on in an uneven manner. I succeeded, even excelled, in some things ... yet floundered in others.

In 1991 I consulted a psychologist. I was becoming desperate. Thinking the cause of my difficulties might be emotional or mental, I decided to try counseling. After listening to me, the doctor startled me when he suggested the cause might be organic and physiological. He ran some simple tests, and told me preliminary results indicated brain dysfunction. He referred me to nearby Roosevelt Warm Springs Rehabilitation Hospital.

After extensive testing, the neurologist there told me that I suffered serious impairment in the right hemisphere of the brain. My memory, too, was affected, especially short-term memory. I had the verbal IQ of a near genius and the short-term memory of someone who was mildly retarded. The likely cause of the memory part of my disability was the head injury.

I reminded the doctors that I had difficulties long before my head injury. They inquired further into my medical history. I told them mine had been a footling breach birth with the cord wrapped around my neck three times and that heavy forceps were used. They speculated that I might have had an initial birth injury that was worsened by the head injury I had in Louisiana.

Normally a diagnosis like mine — organic brain syndrome — would be frightening; for me, though, it was a relief. I had known from my earliest memories I had had puzzling problems, now I knew why. The diagnosis lifted a huge weight of guilt from my shoulders. I wasn't to blame.

> *Christ has not promised us that He will calm every storm in life. But if we come to Him in the midst of our storms and worries, He can calm us.*

More surprises came my way. For years I had been engaged in a ministry as a layman, giving retreats and writing spiritual books. Once the diagnosis was made, I thought it would be a good idea to inform my pastor, Fr. Schreck, about my disability. I trembled a bit, inside, wondering what he would think of me once he knew.

Fr. Schreck listened patiently to me. Then what he said came like a lightening bolt. He didn't say a word about my disability. Instead he looked at me and said firmly, "Eddie, we need to work on getting you ordained, perhaps to the permanent diaconate."

That floored me! "I would have a hard time with the liturgy," I told him.

"Not as a permanent deacon. A deacon can do as much or as little of the liturgy as you are capable. And yet, in the Catholic Church a deacon is a clergyman. Don't you think your ministry here at the parish and throughout the country would go better as a clergyman?"

One Saturday morning, soon after my talk with Fr. Schreck, a call came through from Bishop J. Kevin Boland. He said, "Eddie, we are starting up a permanent diaconate course of studies. You might want to consider applying."

I did, and four and a half years later I found myself lying face down on the floor at John the Baptist as the choir sang the Litany of the Saints at my ordination.

As I lay there on the floor, dressed in an alb, a powerful peace swept through me, body and soul; it was a peace, as the Scriptures say, that surpasses any understanding. I saw how God had been with me even in the roughest spots, how the bright threads of His tender mercies were woven so well into my life. Those childish dreams of my six-year-old self had come true. My desire to be an ordained clergyman had been fulfilled.

Relax in God's Safety

In his letter to the Philippians, Paul speaks of an extraordinary gift of peace that is available to all those who reach for it. Our minds can't understand this peace any more than the eye can hear an orchestra or the ear view a beautiful sunset. The sweetness of His peace, like eternity itself, can be felt, and touched, but never comprehended.

Like a boatman who has struggled against heavy seas can finally relax in the safety and calm peace of the harbor, we are revived when God's peace engulfs us like the warm winds of spring after a bone chilling winter.

"Peace I leave with you." Christ urges His followers in

John's Gospel. "My peace I give to you. I do not give to you as the world gives" [John 14:27]. In the Palestine of Jesus' time, people normally greeted one another with *Shalom,* the Hebrew word meaning "peace be unto you: past, present and future." On Jesus' lips, "Shalom" becomes much more than a simple greeting. The word takes on a new force and depth. As MacLaren said, "On his lips the salutation changes into the tender and mysterious communication of a rare gift."

Christ Calms the Storms of Our Lives

"Shallow water flowing over stones, becomes foamy, disturbed, altered. Yet a deep river flowing over stones stays calm. Deepening our walk with God, is partly how we overcome worries."

ALEXANDER MACLAREN

Christ has not promised us that He will calm every storm in life. But if we come to Him in the midst of our storms and worries, He can calm *us.* As we battle the winds and the tossing waves, below the raging currents of the surface waters can be an unbroken calm of the heart.

Psychologists and medical people offer us fine tools for relaxation, excellent ways for unburdening ourselves; but only prayer can bring true peace of soul. A calm heart mirrors heaven.

 A Calm Heart Mirrors Heaven

PRAYER JOURNEYS

A Prayerful Reading (*Lectio Divina*)

On that day, when evening had come, Jesus said to them,
"Let us go across to the other side."
And leaving the crowd behind,
they took him with them in the boat, just as he was.
Other boats were with him.
A great windstorm arose, and the waves beat into the boat,
so that the boat was already being swamped.
But he was in the stern, asleep on the cushion;
and they woke him up and said to him,
"Teacher, do you not care that we are perishing?"
He woke up and rebuked the wind,
and said to the sea, "Peace! Be still!"
Then the wind ceased, and there was a dead calm.
He said to them, "Why are you afraid?
Have you still no faith?"
And they were filled with great awe
and said to one another, "Who then is this,
that even the wind and the sea obey him?"

(MARK 4:35–41)

A Guided Meditation: *In the Boat with Jesus*

Let the stillness wash over you. God is near you, as near as your breath. You are in another place, another time. You are with Jesus and His disciples, in the scene from Mark you have just read.

Picture yourself in the boat with Jesus and the disciples. The sound of thunder fills your ears. Wind blows raindrops like cold daggers in your face. The boat tosses back and forth from huge waves. You are afraid.

Then the disciples awaken Jesus, and you hear His slow, deep voice call out: "Peace, Be Still." The waves calm. The wind stops. All is calm.

Now in that stillness, imagine Jesus walking over to you in the boat. He softly takes your hand, and his love and peace fill you; your stress begins to leave you. Quietly, in a firm but caring voice, Jesus says, "Peace, Be Still" . . . just to you.

Rest in the calmness a while.

Journal Time

1. Describe a time when a peace from beyond yourself calmed your heart.

2. Write a short prayer thanking God for the times His unexpected peace has helped to calm your life.

"There is the family character in all true Christians, with whatever diversities of idiosyncrasies, and national life or ecclesiastical distinctions. Whether it be St. Francis of Assisi or John Wesley, whether it be Thomas A Kempis or George Fox, the light is one that shines through these many-colored panes of glass. The living Church is the witness of a living Lord, not only before it, and behind it, and above it, but living in it. They are 'light' because they are irradiated by Him. They are 'light' because they are 'in the Lord.' But not only by the fact of the existence of such a community is the witness-bearing effected, but it comes as a personal obligation, with immense weight of pressure and immense possibilities of joy in the discharge of it, to every Christian man and woman."

Alexander MacLaren

12

Moving Beyond Our Stress

"I appeal to you therefore, brethren, by the mercies of God, to present your bodies as a living sacrifice, holy and acceptable to God, which is your spiritual worship."
ROMANS 12:1

ANGELA SPOKE TO ME after an evening's presentation at a parish mission. She told me that recently her prayer life had come to a standstill. Two years earlier, her mother and her niece—with whom she had been especially close— died in a car accident. At first, Angela had been inconsolable; then gradually prayer began to bring her some comfort.

She daily took time for prayerful reading of the Scripture, conversational prayer, and quiet silent prayer.

In the midst of the tumult of her loss, prayer provided consolation, even joy.

Then, after two years, her prayer life changed. Her prayer time became dry, arid as the desert. She rarely felt the presence of God in her daily life. In short, for a while at least, she felt abandoned. Such dry periods in prayer are not uncommon. Holy men and women throughout the history of the Church have at times experienced temporary barriers in their prayer.

Finally, in her quiet times, Angela began to feel somewhat apprehensive about going further in her prayer. She realized something was missing from her life. She felt called to something more, and wasn't sure what it was.

One morning during her prayerful reading of Scripture, she turned to one of her comforting passages in Matthew.

> *"Come to me, all you that are weary and are carrying heavy burdens, and I will give you rest. Take my yoke upon you, and learn from me; for I am gentle and humble in heart, and you will find rest for your souls. For my yoke is easy, and my burden is light"* (MATTHEW 11:28–30).

Her mind usually fixed on the words, "I will give you rest." This time, however, what struck her was, *"Take my yoke upon you, and learn from me."*

"What is Christ's yoke for me?" she thought. It was a moment of insight. During months after the accident, her mind had necessarily been focused on her own need and her family's need for comfort and recovery. Now something different intruded. It was time to move beyond her loss, and to follow Christ anew in discipleship.

This had been the source of her apprehension: She had sensed that if she continued to pray, it would lead her to change, to reach outward. Quickly Angela turned to other parts of the Scriptures. She turned to the account of Christ washing the feet of the disciples. The passage that spoke to her heart, that she softly repeated over and over again, read,

"So, if I, your Lord and Teacher have washed your feet, you also ought to wash one another's feet. For I have set you an example that you should do as I have done to you. Very truly, I tell you, servants are not greater than their master, nor are messengers greater than the one who sent them. If you know these things, you are blessed if you do them"

(JOHN 13:14–17).

Silently Angela prayed, "Lord, you have been washing my feet, now it's time for me to begin ministering to those who need comfort, in the way you have comforted me."

She began thinking of a neighbor who had just lost her sister. *I can take time to be with her,* Angela thought. She began to think of other ways she could touch people in her congregation that had recently experienced loss. She spoke to her pastor about starting a grief support group. Her background in social work had given her skills to lead such groups. The pastor immediately said yes.

As she began listening to others who had lost loved ones and lending them support, Angela no longer noticed whether her prayer times were full of consolation or not. Her mind was focused on others. She loved reading spiritual and theological books, and also became involved with teaching adult education at her parish. Enthusiasm and energy returned to her life. One Sunday afternoon as she laughed and played in a park with her husband and children, she felt the joy of life course through her. She had followed Christ's example, and had begun to live her life for others.

What Is Your Next Step?

> *The rest Christ calls us to does far more than bring tranquility. It calls us to walk alongside Him, to engage in His work in the world.*

From the medieval Church comes an illustration of how prayer can become a costly but positive addiction. There was once a wine merchant who gave out free samples of wonderful-tasting, rare wine. As his customers developed a taste for the great wine, he charged a small amount for the wine. A short time later, he increased the price gradually, until the wine became very costly. At last his customers began to sell all their possessions to buy the fine-tasting wine.

So it is with God's presence in prayer. At first it comes without obligation, then when we become addicted to that love, we willingly give our whole lives to Him in discipleship. But unlike the merchant in the story, the sweet wine our Savior gives us, His very life, is an "addiction" that leads to our only true source of freedom and eternal life.

Let's look once more at the passage in Matthew 11:

> *"Take my yoke upon you, and learn from me …*
> *For my yoke is easy, and my burden is light."*

The rest Christ calls us to does far more than bring

tranquility. It calls us to walk alongside Him, to engage in His work in the world. Taking His yoke upon ourselves, we are led to imitate Him as Christ binds us to himself.

Christ's peace is a costly peace.

When Jesus said, "my yoke is *easy*," He did not mean that we would never again have to exert ourselves. The Greek word that is translated "easy," *chrestos*, means well-fitting.

The yokes in Jesus day were made to fit the ox. A carpenter would hew each yoke to fit a particular animal so that the yoke would not hurt the ox or cause sores. It was tailor-made, so to speak.

Similarly, when we let Christ lift our burdens, when we journey into His rest, we are invited to take up His work with and for Him, to live our lives for Him, to go out of ourselves to love and serve others. His call upon us is unique.

"It is not the burden is easy to carry,
but it is laid out for us in love;
it is meant to be carried in love.
And love makes the heaviest burdens light"
WILLIAM BARCLAY

The rest Christ gives us is costly; it costs our lives. When we say "yes" to His rest, we say "yes" to His call for us to go beyond ourselves. It means loving those He loves, and caring about those things that are on His heart. The more we pray and the closer we draw to Christ, the more we love like he loves and the stronger the call comes to surrender our lives to him. We grow to love the weak, the disabled, the poorest of the poor, victims of injustice, all those Christ loves so fervently.

By taking up our yoke, we begin to spread the good news of His love to others in our actions and in our words. We allow prayer to so saturate our personalities that our very presence brings peace and calm to others. As we are calmed and comforted by Christ, we can be transfigured until the very tone of our voices, the peace in our faces, can calm and comfort others.

Lord, you comfort me that I may comfort others. You draw near to me that I may spread your love.

Lord, you comfort me that I may comfort others.
You draw near to me that I may spread your love.
In the sending of the Spirit upon simple fishermen,
You have cast out a net that has netted the whole world.
Help me to cast out my nets
and respond with a yes to your call for me to become a
disciple.
Take me beyond myself, beyond my personal needs,
help me to lose myself in loving others.
Guide me in loving like you love,
Help me care for the things you care about,
washing the feet of others as you have washed my feet.

PRAYER JOURNEYS
A Prayerful Reading *(Lection Divina)*

Jesus, knowing that the Father had given
all things into his hands,
and that he had come from God and was going to God,
got up from the table, took off his outer robe,
and tied a towel around himself.
Then he poured water into a basin
and began to wash the disciples' feet and to wipe them
with the towel that was tied around him.
He came to Simon Peter, who said to him,
"Lord, are you going to wash my feet?"
Jesus answered, "You do not know now what I am doing,
but later you will understand."
Peter said to him, "You will never wash my feet."
Jesus answered, "Unless I wash you,
you have no share with me."
Simon Peter said to him, "Lord, not my feet only
but also my hands and my head!"
Jesus said to him, "One who has bathed
does not need to wash,
except for the feet, but is entirely clean..."
After he had washed their feet, had put on his robe,
and had returned to the table he said to them,
"Do you know what I have done to you?
You call me Teacher and Lord—and you are right,
for that is what I am.

So if I, your Lord and Teacher, have washed your feet,
you also ought to wash one another's feet.
For I have set you an example,
that you should do as I have done to you. Very truly,
I tell you,
servants are not greater than their master,
nor are messengers greater than the one who sent them.
If you know these things, you are blessed if you do them."

JOHN 13:3–10, 12–17

A Guided Meditation: *Washing One Another's Feet*

Sit in a comfortable chair. Let your mind and body grow still. God's love is all around you, comforting, consoling and reassuring you. Perhaps say the Jesus Prayer for a while, letting the prayer deepen the stillness.

You become aware of someone entering the room. It is Jesus. He has a towel wrapped around Him, and is carrying a basin of water. The soft heavenly light that surrounds Him now surrounds you, deepening your stillness. The light caresses you, touches you, and heals you.

Jesus kneels down in front of you. Slowly He takes off your shoes and socks. He begins tenderly washing your feet with the towel and basin of warm water. The soft, warm touch of the towel on your feet becomes a conduit of Jesus' love for you. That love softens your heart, reminding you how special you are to Jesus.

When He finishes, Jesus stays there for a few moments in the stillness. Let that stillness sink deep within you. Then He says to you, almost in a whisper: "I have set you an example, that you should do as I have done to you." Then He stands, hands you the basin and the towel, and steps aside.

There is now an empty chair in front of you, facing you. You sense what Jesus wants you to do. He wants you to wash other people's feet. Who are the people you are especially called to serve? One by one, see them seated in the chair with bare feet. With thankfulness and humility, wash their feet in the way Jesus has washed your feet.

Journal Time

1. Intercessory prayer is a wonderful way to pray, drawing us beyond ourselves. Who especially needs your prayers right now? Write out a prayer for that person, then read it aloud slowly and prayerfully.

2. Christ's yoke is "well-fitting," made for each of us individually. What particular ministry or service to others do you feel is particularly well-fitting for you? Write about it.

APPENDIX ONE:

Prayer Experience and Verse Index

147

"Do not let your hearts be troubled. Believe in God, believe also in me." John 14:1–3 (3)

"Do not worry about anything, but in everything by prayer and supplication with thanksgiving let your requests be made known to God." Philippians 4:6–7 (5, 7, 9, 11)

"Every valley shall be lifted up, and every mountain and hill be made low . . ." Isaiah 40:4 (4)

"Father, into your hands I commend my spirit." Luke 23:46 (2)

"For as we share abundantly in Christ's sufferings ..." 2 Corinthians 1:5 (2)

Giving and Getting Forgiveness: A Guided Meditation (6)

"God, be merciful to me, a sinner." Luke 18:13 (2)

"God is our refuge and strength, a very present help in trouble." Psalm 46:1–3 (3)

"He said to them, 'Why are you afraid? Have you no faith?'" Mark 5:40 (4)

"He who brings thanksgiving as his sacrifice honors me; to him who orders his way aright I will show the salvation of God!" Psalm 50:23 (10)

How to Pray the Jesus Prayer (2)

"How sweet are your words to my taste, sweeter than honey to my mouth!" Psalm 119:103 (3)

"I appeal to you therefore, brethren, by the mercies of God, to present your bodies as a living sacrifice, holy and acceptable to God, which is your spiritual worship." Romans 12:1 (12)

"I come to the Garden alone, while the dew is still on the roses . . ." (4)

"I have loved you with an everlasting love; I have drawn you with loving-kindness." Jeremiah 31:3 (5)

"If I speak in the tongues of mortals and of angels, but do not have love ..." 1 Corinthians 13:1–13 (6)

"If the LORD had not been my help, my soul would soon have dwelt in the land of silence." Psalm 94:17 (10)

In the Boat with Jesus: A Guided Meditation (11)

"It is in vain that you rise up early and go late to rest ... for he gives to his beloved sleep." Psalm 127:2 (8)

"Jesus is Lord, to the glory of God the Father." Philippians 2:11 (2)

"Jesus, knowing that the father had given all things into his hands ..." John 13:3–10 (12)

"Jesus, Son of David, have mercy on me." Luke 18:38 (2)

"Let the same mind be in you that was in Christ Jesus ..." Philippians 1:3–5 (2)

Light of the Risen Christ: A Guided Prayer Journey (5)

"Look at the birds of the air; they neither sow nor reap nor gather into barns, and yet your heavenly Father feeds them." Matthew 6:26 (4)

Lord, You comfort me that I may comfort others. (12)

Lord, Your abundance fills the universe. Your love can fill the crevices of my soul. (9)

Lord Jesus, You are more intimate to us than we are to ourselves. (5)

"The LORD is the everlasting God, the Creator of the ends of the earth." Isaiah 40:28 (4)

"The LORD upholds all who are falling, and raises up all who are bowed down." Psalm 145:14 (9)

"The sacrifice acceptable to God is a broken spirit ..." Psalm 51:17 (6)

"Therefore I tell you, do not worry about your life ..." Matthew 6:25–34 (7)

"Thou dost keep him in perfect peace, whose mind is stayed on thee..." Isaiah 25:3 (11)

Touch of Comfort: A Guided Meditation (7)

Washing One Another's Feet: A Guided Meditation (12)

"We know that in everything God works for good with those who love him ..." Romans 8:28 (8, 9)

"When you pass through the waters, I will be with you ..." Isaiah 43:2 (1, 9)

Appendix Two:
Prayer Experts Listed

Alexander MacLaren was a Baptist contemplative and founding president of the Baptist World Alliance in the late 1800,s. Large crowds came to hear him preach and he was called one of the "great expositors" of Scripture. He quoted the Church Fathers and Catholic sources on spirituality as well as his own Protestant and Biblical sources. He often spoke of contemplation and meditation in words that still speak to the hearts of both Protestants and Catholics alike.

Alphonsus de Liguori: The patron saint of Conversational Prayer, lived in Italy during the eighteenth century. Wrote *Prayer As Conversing with God as a Friend*.

Augustine of Hippo (4th century): Author of *Confessions*, one of the greatest spiritual autobiographies of all time.

Bernard of Clairvaux (12th century): Cistercian monk, mystic, and Church Father well known for his sermons on the Song of Songs and other books in Scripture.

Biblical Illustrator: A huge, multi-volume Protestant nineteenth century commentary on Scripture written as a source for sermons.

Canon Miller: 19th century Anglican clergyman.

Corrie Ten Boom: Dutch Evangelist whose family was incarcerated in the Nazi concentration camps of World War II. After the war, she traveled throughout the world with the message of God's love and forgiveness—despite having lost most of her immediate family in the camps.

Cyril of Jerusalem (4th Century): Bishop of Jerusalem and fighter of heresy.

Edward Halowell: A Christian psychiatrist who teaches at Harvard Medical School, calls constant worry "a disease of the imagination."

Edward Perronet (1779): Wrote "All Hail the Power of Jesus' Name," he was a British Protestant minister in the late 1700's and a close associate of the founder of the Methodist movement, John Wesley.

Elizabeth Ann Seton: 18th century convert to the Catholic faith, she is the first American-born canonized saint.

Henry Ward Beecher: Evangelical preacher of 19th century.

John of Kronstadt (d.1908): An expressive and impressive preacher, a promoter of frequent communion, this Russian Orthodox priest moved the hearts of hardened sinners to repentance, a man with a great depth of love, and a spiritual healer.

Luke Dysinger, O.S.B: This Benedictine monk teaches marriage and human sexuality, bioethics, patristics, and the history of Christian spirituality at Saint John's Seminary in Camarillo, and the history of Christian spirituality at Loyola-Marymount University.

Pope Benedict XVI (formerly Joseph Cardinal Ratzinger). Quote taken from audience on November 16, 2005.

Rosalind Rinker: Former Protestant missionary to China and expert on Conversational Prayer. Her work influenced the widely used Catholic Bible study called the Little Rock Bible Study.

Walter Brueggemann: Professor emeritus of Old Testament at Columbia Theological Seminary in Decatur, Georgia.

Way of the Pilgrim: Written by an anonymous, lame and destitute Russian peasant in the 19th century. Over the years this book became a spiritual classic on the Jesus Prayer that sells well even today.

APPENDIX THREE:

Resources for Further Study

A Monk of the Eastern Church. The Jesus Prayer (Crestwood, NY: St. Vladimir's Press, 1987).

Alphonsus de Liguori, Selected Writings (Mahwah, NJ: Paulist Press, 1999).

Bernard of Clairvaux. On The Song of Songs, Vol. I (Kalamazoo, MI: Cistercian Publications, 1976).

Bernard of Clairvaux. On The Song of Songs Vol. II (Kalamazoo, MI: Cistercian Publications, 1976).

Colbert, Don, MD. Stress Less (Lake Mary, FL: Siloam, 2005).

Hallowell, Edward M., MD. Worry (New York, NY: Random House, 1997).

Hybels, Bill. Too Busy Not To Pray (Downers Grove, IL: InterVarsity Press, 1998).

Rinker, Rosalind. Learning Conversational Prayer (Collegeville, MN: The Liturgical Press, 1992).

Would You Like Deacon Eddie to Speak to Your Parish or Other Group?

Deacon Eddie Ensley and Deacon Robert Herrmann speak at parish missions, retreats, and conferences throughout the United States. Their Christ-centered parish missions draw everyone together, recharging the congregation as they rediscover important things like wonder, mystery and prayer. People reconcile. Faith is awakened. Vocations are discovered. Families are healed. Lives are forever changed. The parish discovers afresh its ultimate calling and meaning. A Parish Mission is a MUST. Why? Because nothing less than miracles can happen! Miracles of the heart!

Consider inviting Deacon Eddie to talk with your parish or other group about important topics such as …

- The art of prayer—meeting God in authentic conversation.
- How to deal with the tough issues of life.
- Contemplative prayer is for everyone.
- Healing relationships.
- Transforming anger and bitterness through compassion.
- Healing past hurts.
- How life's losses can become steppingstones to new beginnings.
- How to forgive from the heart.
- Embracing the unconditional love of God.
- Recognizing the sacred moments of our lives.

For more information
Email: pmissions@charter.net

NOTES

NOTES

NOTES

About the Author

 EDDIE ENSLEY is the author of numerous books, including the bestselling *Prayer that Heals Our Emotions*. As a clergyman and pastoral counselor with a graduate degree in pastoral studies from Loyola University, he writes with sensitivity to the broad Christian community, including Protestants, Catholics, and Orthodox. Ensley conducts retreats throughout the country, and is known for his ability to make spiritual practices accessible to the average person. You can contact him at pmissions@charter.net